*'A man with one watch knows what time it is;
a man with two watches is never quite sure.'*

Lee Segalln

The watchmaker, painting by Josef Urban, 19th century

Thomas M. Meine
Matthew Stannard

COLLECTING (VINTAGE) WATCHES

Wristwatches, antique- and vintage pocket watches

1970s OMEGA F300 tuning fork wristwatch

Bibliographic information published by the Deutsche Nationalbibliothek:

The Deutsche Nationalbibliothek lists this publication in the Deutsche Nationalbibliografie; detailed bibliographic data are available on the Internet at http://dnb.dnb.de

Manufactured and published by
BoD - Books on Demand, Norderstedt
All rights reserved

Copyright © Thomas M. Meine, Matthew Stannard

May 2021

ISBN 9 783744 894920

CONTENTS

	Page
Watches shown in the book	7
Collecting (vintage) watches	9
Watches and time	19
The quartz crisis and the revival of the mechanical watches	27
Radium contamination	30
Clocking of watches, corresponding amplitudes	31
Time – one of the standard units	37
Mechanical wristwatches, hand wind	41
Watch cases	58
Shock protection	59
Compensating balance, screw balance	60
Magnetism and watches	61
Adjustment and regulation of a watch	65
Condition of watch dials	68
Mechanical wristwatches, automatic	69
TIMEX, new techniques	77
TIMEX watches, mechanical, hand wind	82
TIMEX watches, mechanical, automatic	83
TIMEX, 1. Electric watches, 2. Electronic watches, 3. Quartz controlled electric watches	84
Tuning fork watches	88
Quartz controlled tuning fork watches	91
Quartz watches	93
SWATCH	100
Radio controlled watches	103
Antique and vintage pocket watches	106
Watch movements – the gold rush	144

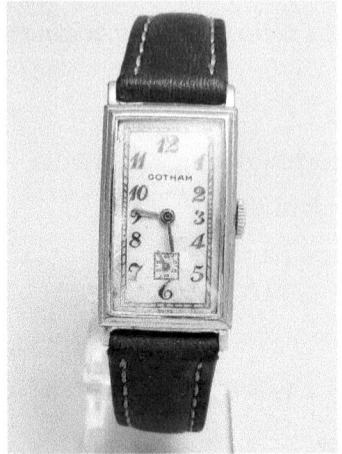

1947 Gotham wristwatch by **Ollendorf**, Switzerland and USA

Verge fusee pocket watch, England, between 1750 and 1780

WATCHES SHOWN IN THE BOOK

The watches presented in this book, with a small selection of tools and equipment added, can only cover a mere fraction of the different timepieces as they came along over time. No museum would have the space to display every variation that was ever made. Different types of watches have been grouped together as far as possible. If you are missing some of your favorite brands, bear in mind, that these images have all been taken from original watches as they were available. Some specific images, not self-produced, have been marked as such or are in public domain.

When putting this all together, the core focus was set on the largest possible coverage of the different techniques and types of watches as they have appeared over time, still available and affordable today within a reasonable budget, rather than on a few highly-priced specimens. This, of course, must also include watches which are less attractive to the ambitious collector, but are nevertheless an indispensable part of the overall picture.

Seen from this angle, a mass product like an Elgin mechanical pocket watch, a Timex electric, a Bulova tuning fork watch plus a Far East quartz watch, as an exemplary selection, will tell more about watchmaking, than a single luxury timepiece with a hammer price of US $50.000 at Sotheby's, although the latter would certainly be nice to have.

There are specialized exhibitions or locations displaying precious watches, interesting also from a technical and historical point of view. But too often, you will find places with motley assortments of gorgeous clocks and watches – gorgeous in a sense of their fancy external appearance. What's really more important is the technique behind and the art of watchmaking implemented *inside* these fascinating little machines.

I rather stare all day at John Harrison's 'H4' marine chronometer in the National Maritime Museum, Greenwich, a watch which has changed the course of our world by finally solving the problem of calculating longitude while at sea, then five minutes at some fire gilded, distasteful Louis XVI fireplace clocks, where the craftsmanship went into the sculptures and bric-a-brac above and around the clock in line with contemporary liking and not primarily into the movement and its precision.

But that's unfortunately true for a large variety of watches and clocks throughout history. Whenever a certain technical stage was reached, believed to be sufficient for the needs of the time, 'creativity' went in different directions, like material, embellishments of all sorts, mostly superfluous complications or useless gimmicks. Posh dials often make it difficult to see what time it is, and some fatal and mysterious road accidents might find an explanation by examining the driver's watch with its artistically designed and hard to read dial.

Above left: Henlein-Watch (named after Peter Henlein). The Henlein watch is a drum watch, also called Nuremberg Egg, made in 1510, on display in the Germanic National Museum, Nuremberg. **Above right: a replica of a portable sun-dial.**

Left: Royal Observatory, Greenwich, printing from 1833.

Greenwich is the home of the Prime Meridian, where West meets East at the longitude 0°. At noon, it also divides the world into equally long a.m. and p.m. timespans. The International Date Line lies exactly on the opposite side, at 180° longitude. It is a very practical location, as there are only very few people in that area in the Pacific Ocean, having to live with the problem that close neighbors have a different date. Greenwich Mean Time (GMT) was the world time standard until 1972. It was subsequently replaced by UTC (Universal Time Coordinated). GMT still has the same time as UTC, but has since then become a pure time zone.

Due to the overall slowing down of the Earth's rotation, time has to be periodically adjusted, which is reflected in the UTC. When 25 nations met in Washington DC in the year 1884 to decide on the location of the Prime Meridian, Greenwich was selected, mainly because already chosen by the USA. The vote was 22 : 1, with two abstentions coming from France and Brazil and one vote against from San Domingo *(who?)*. The line of the Prime Meridian has meanwhile been moved 102.5 meters to the East, due to new satellite data and other measurements. It is now called IRM (International Reference Meridian) and puts the observatory and the historic Prime Meridian to the West of it. Interesting: The Eurasian plate, including the Royal Observatory, is slowly drifting further away north-east, approximately 2.5cm per year – about the annual growing rate of your fingernails. The IRM is not fixed to any specific point on Earth anymore.

COLLECTING (VINTAGE) WATCHES

Before things tend to get out of hand, always remember a wise saying, coined by someone whose name I unfortunately forgot: *"in the time you spend collecting things, better take a walk instead"*.

Is it a good and wise thing to collect (vintage) watches in larger quantities? There are two answers to this question; a clear and definite *'yes'* and a decisive *'no'* – and everything in between.

Yes, by all means! – because watches are fascinating little machines with an exciting history. They have accompanied mankind since a long time, have driven forward also other technical developments and revolutionized the world. They are, still today, representing the finest in engineering and craftsmanship and have always been fun to have and wear.

No, what for? – because they have become more and more superfluous, as time is available everywhere and at higher precision than what can be achieved by a mechanical watch. The chairman of an upper luxury watch brand has recently stated that they sell products no one needs at luxury prices, and that was meant to be a selling argument, certainly putting some specific people above the crowd.

And it is naturally also a matter of money spent and quantities, from a few specimens to piles of ticking friends and room-filling accumulations.

Why people collect watches, especially in large, occasionally sprawling quantities, can not so easily be explained, not even with a 'collecting mania', which would not be different from other 'accumulations' of particular objects.

Not too long ago, the average family did not have more than one or two timekeepers, a pendulum clock on the wall or a desk clock, and a pocket watch to be carried to work. More than today, people have adapted to the natural daily routine. Private activities, especially in times without television and the Internet, have been totally different and were to a lesser extent been governed by temporary fashion. However, one was mostly on time, something which is proving to be more difficult for some of today's contemporaries.

One thing is for sure, if seen from a strictly financial point of view: with certain exceptions – primarily in the luxury sector – and if not professionally done (which would also involve frequent selling and letting go at the right moment) – watches and clocks are amongst the worst investments one can make on this planet.

Getting rid of watches again, especially in larger quantities and in a short space of time, can mostly be done only under painful losses; and often, the *'ticking friends'* come back to the market for a song, at garage sales or 'from estate'.

As a collector, mostly tempted to pay the highest price, it is good to keep things within reasonable bounds. You should accept that money is lost, like after a good dinner or a visit to the Opera, with the exception, that the watches will still be there

to enjoy, with whatever residual value. To determine quickly what's lost at the very moment you are about to greedily buy a watch, think of going to the next store or the next auction and imagine a realistic price you will be able to obtain. If your imagination suggests enormous profits, you are destined for a very harsh landing on the grounds of reality. The only way to make a sure profit is to steal or inherit a watch.

So, what's motivating a collector?

It must be the fascination for the technique, especially of the mechanical versions of the timepieces, perhaps also the interest in the individual stages of development or the allure of some particular models.

For the male part of the population, it has always been – and still is – a piece of jewelry a *man* can wear, notwithstanding the fact that even tax-advisors can nowadays run around with a nose-ring or piercings of all sorts. Occasionally, it is also a signal to the personal environment – of whatever nature – a status symbol or a form of self-expression.

But in the end, things must lie much deeper. It is the time which is within all of us, which 'governs' us, which occasionally even makes us – often unconsciously – feel uncanny. We only get a small portion of it, not knowing how much and all associated with the uncertainty about what comes after. As much as we have to concentrate on hours and minutes to respect plans or to timely attend certain events, it is always the time in its larger dimension which stands above everything.

Nature does not know us and doesn't care what we, a flyspeck in the system, do or don't. Everything follows physical law in the endless universe, beyond the limit of human comprehension. Time is running out on this planet anyway, as we will learn in more detail in a later chapter. We can only speed up the end of mankind locally, without any influence overall, but we can measure tiny fractions of the time, even on our wrist.

While some collectors love the different types of clocks, it's certainly the pocket- and wristwatches which account for the largest part of the collections.

Many people don't even know that they collect watches. One should really count all the watches which have accumulated over time, lying around, often unused. If all devices are also added which are no watches or clocks, but include and also indicate the time, like a microwave oven, the TV set, a recorder, a camera, a smartphone and what have you, fifty or more 'watches' are often around people which would not consider themselves as watch collectors.

Collecting watches has always been popular. They can be new or old, for daily use or just kept in a box or safe. For new mechanical watches, prices of US $5,000, US $25,000 or even US $250,000 are nothing exceptional and often precious material of the case, the bracelet or a setting with diamonds are only partly determining the price-level.

US $1,000 is rather at the lower end than in the middle segment of renowned brands; in the premium sector, this would be very far away even from the entry level. Super-complications (watches with numerous, in particular rare indications above a moon phase, perpetual calendar, etc.), combined with exclusive names, can carry extremely hefty price tags, and there are almost no limits when two rich people quarrel about who of them has the best watch and privately commission new models with ever more complications, most of them totally useless or impractical, like many of those implemented in more household watches.

Used mechanical wristwatches of a particular kind can occasionally see a hammer price at auctions of several million US Dollars plus premium and VAT. The high bids mostly come over telephone, when the buyers want to stay in the hiding for obvious reasons. At the same time, they avoid the danger of being personally identified some day on the pillory of crazy collectors. But it needs only two bidders with enough money, fighting over one item, to catch the virus and to lose control.

All in all, what concerns prices paid, I guess this is just another bubble which is inevitably destined to burst. But even watches, more in the budget of the 'normal' collector, are fetching ever higher (sometimes idiotic) prices, on Internet platforms or elsewhere, until also this craziness will go up in smoke, sooner or later – at least based on the real value of money and not in nominal terms of some rotten currency like the Euro.

Specialization is a good thing, but not a must, unless an impressive number of timepieces harvested is the intended main characteristic of a collection. But even then, do not go for ruined, half-dead or optically and hygienically repulsive watches, unless you need parts, objects of practice or have other plausible reasons. A clean watch in working condition is worth a lot more than a pile of such junk.

The more you know about a watch in your collection, the better. It also increases the value for a collector, a big advantage if the watch is to be sold some day. This includes maker, movement, age, specific technical details, materials, etc. Some people don't even know how to correctly set the date or other indications on the vintage watch they have acquired, often the cause of damage done to delicate components. Original documents and boxes add to the value, but that is a criterion (and proof of origin) for expensive timepieces, otherwise just nice to have. You might also look for odd things in whatever area of vintage timepieces, go for a particular brand, a certain period, or concentrate on unusual characteristics. Exclusivity must not solely be determined by the price or the trend.

Older watches are divided into antique (older than 100 years) or vintage (they should have an age of at least 25 years, preferably 30 or more; the borders are not so clearly defined). They have been produced and sold in the billions, but specimens, even from mass production, in pristine or mint condition, are naturally getting ever rarer, especially as lots of them have been neglected over time or have never seen a regular professional service.

There is an important element to remember when collecting watches, especially the mechanical type, regularly worn or not. Even when unused, they need a regular service as the oils inside will dry out over time. They are still working, but the dried-in oils will work like sandpaper on shafts and bearings when the watch is running. So, service costs add up over time, but a lot of collectors say *'so what, that's cents a day, spread over a period of several years, and the joy it gives is worth a lot more!'* That's certainly right for *one* watch and exclusive watches can become really costly – per piece!

Now, you might want to know how often a watch has to be given away to get a service. The answer to that is not so easy. It depends on many factors, type, age, use; etc. It's also a question of 'just' a service – disassembly, cleaning, oiling, re-assembly and adjustment – or if some repair is needed. Figures in the ballpark range from 2 to 10 years, whereby things have changed somewhat with the new types of oils used, having a much longer durability.

And then, there is that strange phenomena which can be observed in this connection: service intervals always get much shorter towards the lower end when people give an advice to others, and move opposite to the longer end, when it comes to service their own watches.

Occasionally, one can find so-called NOS (New Old Stock, new watches from old stock). They come up from inventory of the manufacturers, have been forgotten at a watchmaker's- or jeweler's place, have been pure and unused collector's items (although in this case they should not be called as such) or are simply faked or cobbled together from old parts.

'NOS', 'pristine' or 'mint', one has to wonder what some people think these terms exactly mean when it comes to offering watches on Internet sales platforms, often for specimens even far away from an average state of preservation. And a lot of people do not have a clue when something comes along as 'minty'. That means 'cool' at the very best (if not used in a totally different context in local slang).

Talking about Internet sales platforms: It takes a lot of experience to 'read' and interpret the offers correctly.

Missing details, bad images, no idea about age and maker, no movement pictures, not even an indication about what's inside, scarce and incomplete or even false descriptions, can be a hint that the seller might be honest, but has no inkling of what he is selling – often a source for a bargain buy, but mostly this is a signal to stay away as far as possible.

If you offer a watch at whatever price, you should really know what you are trying to sell (perhaps with the help of an expert or watchmaker) and provide a minimum of information as well as clear and meaningful images. And especially in the higher priced categories, *'runs, not tested for accuracy'* is a no-go.

It must not be a test on the timegrapher (see page 36), but winding up and setting the watch, checking how much it is slow or fast after 24 hours and how long it ran (power reserve), can be done by a 10-year-old child.

Whatever, people fall into apparent traps, day after day. *No movement shot – no purchase*, should be the rule, unless other convincing elements or an extremely low price justify putting up a bid.

The list of fakes and imitations in circulation is endless. That begins with total forgeries, faked or badly restored dials (specialist term 're-dial') or badly repaired originals with all sorts of parts not compatible with the original. The *'franken-watches'* (named after the monster created by Dr. Frankenstein), patched up from bits and pieces of different watches, are an inherent part of the market for vintage watches.

Besides private tinkerers, there are entire industries which have been established around the faking and *'frankening'* of watches. We can see downright nauseating forgeries of famous brands or dreadfully re-dialed originals coming from India, the so-called *'Mumbai-specials'* (usually still referred to as *'Bombay-specials'*).

There are several places around the world which a vintage watch collector, especially the inexperienced, should avoid like the plaque.

In the Ukraine, a lot of efforts are put into fumbling around in the glut of Russian watches which come back to the market as *'franked'* bits and pieces with fake dials, etc. If you want the Czar of Russia with his daughter Anastasia on his lap or counterfeit emblems of the Wehrmacht (or worse) on the face of an old pocket watch, this is the place to get them. Naturally, you will also find honest dealers in the Ukraine; it's just a matter of identifying them – the needle in the haystack.

The French, with their nice, melodious and dulcet language, giving even toilet articles a special touch, have their own 'word of exclusivity' for watches which have been cobbled together: *'marriage'* (marriage).

Then, there are these cheap products, mostly coming from that large country in the Far East, or have at least been produced there, with formerly big names on the dial. Often, just the name rights have been acquired of companies which went out of business a long time ago, caused by the quartz crisis or for other reasons. Today's products have no relation to the old shop whatsoever and certainly no uninterrupted historical connection.

The advertising *'since 1850'* might be correct in a legal sense concerning the name, a serious buyer can however only laugh about this nonsense. If a website of such a company should exist at all, then one too often does not find an appropriate masthead or even a simple contact address. Conclusion: Better no watch than this garbage. Admittedly, things are more and more moving into the right direction what concerns the quality 'Made in China' – be it the trash can on one side and serious business on the other end.

In addition, we have new products with freshly created, often ridiculous names. As an advertising man, I could extend the list of these hot-air brands with names like, *'Worldman and Sons'*, *'Prince of England'*, *'Mayflower'*, *'Zeppelin'*, *'Nicewear'*, *'Shinebright Watch'*, *'Bravesmart'* or *'King Time'*. And yes, there are all the *'misspelled'* names on the dial, slightly variating from well know brand names, looking for idiots to spend their money on this rubbish.

Whatever, if you are only interest in knowing what time it is at a given moment, you are well served with a cheap quartz watch – almost irrelevant where it comes from, and if you stay below or near the cost for a battery change, you can simply throw it away when the time has come (of course observing environmental regulations). But there are also not so cheap and excellent quartz watches out there, both in quality and appearance, most definitively worth wearing and collecting.

And then, we have the hordes of 'restorers', amateurs and occasionally also professionals who, despite best intentions, screw up on watch-restorations, worse than someone giving an inherited 18th century piece of furniture a new shine with blue gloss paint. Here, we can observe a never tiring 'effort' to make well-preserved watches steadily rarer.

Someone has once stated, that every idiot can make (or better, have someone make) expensive watches, if he has the financial means and a good marketing concept. That also high quality, precision, precious materials and the mastery of technical challenges must be associated with this endeavor is out of the question – only the prices are sometimes far away from being in any sensible proportion to the real value.

It is, however, something totally different to produce watches for the mass market which everyone can afford as reliable companions in day-to-day life.

Timex, still very active today, has produced *one billion* watches between 1950 and 1980 alone. That means more than 130,000 pieces every working day. They are still available at affordable prices, although specimens in top condition are ever harder to come by, because Timex watches were made to wear, not to collect. For the collector with an interest in the technical development of watchmaking, Timex also made numerous electric- and electronic watches, the first models to have batteries inside, replacing the main spring as a source of power.

Of course, many other producers have also supplied the mass markets with affordable, yet reliable watches which the collector can get for cheap money. Perhaps a good occasion for the beginner to start a collection or to fill up the rows in a collection of a quantity-oriented hoarder of timepieces.

Leaving aside all the different kinds of clocks, we are looking at portable watches which have been made from the 16th century until today. Wristwatches had been smaller pocket watches in the early beginning, which were somehow attached to the wrist. Later, they got their typical shape and type of lugs to fasten wristbands.

The watch on the wrist was more practical under many aspects, especially in the upcoming Industrial Age. There was less interruption of the work when people wanted to quickly check the time. Simultaneously, ideas went into all directions, like designing watches which were easier to read depending on the activities of the wearer, like watches for chauffeurs with curved cases and crystals, making it possible to check the time without taking the hands off the steering wheel.

Particular watches are produced for nurses who, for hygienic reasons, are often not allowed to carry wristwatches at work, especially in sensitive areas. The dial of these watches, hanging on the scrubs like a medal, is inserted upside down and can be checked from above when lifted up.

The so-called 'trench-watches' are very popular and sought after by collectors. The military in WW I carried them in the trenches. Normal pocket watches were impractical, when the elbow-room was limited, especially when wearing thick clothing and carrying equipment. There was a higher danger that the watches got damaged or that the crystal was broken, that's why a genuine trench-watch is characterized by a metal grill or mesh that covers and protects the crystal, but still allows reading the time. These covers are often referred to as 'shrapnel guard', but they would have certainly been useless if the watch and its wearer were hit by shrapnel, but are certainly a good shield against bumps and knocks in such cramped conditions.

Another sort of watch, from a long list of different types, are the so-called 'divers' (divers' watch). They have a very solid, waterproof case, with special seals for the crown and pushers. A characteristic feature is the rotating bezel, which allows controlling the diving-time. It should be rotatable only in one direction: counter-clockwise (!). This way, an accidental setting change would indicate a shorter diving time left and not a longer, if moved clockwise – with possibly very severe consequences. As this type of bezels looks nice on a watch, they often come as mere decorations on all sorts of timepieces. Nevertheless, also quality brand names come with divers and a bezel that rotates bi-directional, but I am sure, these watches are basically just left on the wrist under the shower, in the pool or during snorkeling, but not during serious diving in demanding environments.

Good divers' watches are resistant to a pressure of a few hundred meters under water and far beyond. They can even come with a helium valve (helium escape valve). This is a security valve through which helium can escape from the case. Without this device, saturation divers had occasionally observed that the watch crystal was blown off during the decompression phase due to the overpressure inside the watch. During the diving activities, the breathing air is enriched with helium gas. Its particles are the smallest found in nature and can penetrate even through tight gaskets and then cannot get out again fast enough. Whatever, most of these watches will mostly just be worn under the shower and never see a depth below 2 meters in the pool.

Chronographs are also in high demand. They have a start- and stop mechanism (stop-watch feature) to measure time intervals with corresponding sub-dials. The large seconds hand can either be used for the Chrono-function with a de-central seconds indication or as the normal seconds hand and the Chrono-seconds are shown in a small, separate dial. Other sub-dials count minutes and hours. A white main-dial with black sub-dials is called a Panda-dial (like the white face of a Panda Bear with black circles around the eyes). The other way around, horologists speak of a reverse Panda-dial, an inversion of the Panda's face.

They are attractive watches, reflecting the highest art of watchmaking, but they are the costliest when it comes to pay for a routine service (not to speak of repairs). This stop-mechanism is more for the pleasure to *'interact'* with the watch – a meaner expression would be *'playing around'*. Naturally, they run very precisely, but do not even come near to a specially designed, even cheap stop-watch what concerns manageability and practicability, but are certainly nice to have.

Chronograph and Chronometer are terms which are often mixed up. A chronograph is a watch with a stop-watch feature; a chronometer is a very accurately running watch with a high-grade movement, certified by standard laboratories, like today by the Swiss COSC (Contrôle Officiel Suisse des Chronomètres).

We should leave it at this still incomplete inventory of variants. The list would otherwise become too long.

Ladies' watches across the board are valued much cheaper as vintage collector's watches – to be honest, no one really wants them. They are practically of no interest to the male collector. Especially in past times, they came too small and in their typical style. Technically they are usually kept rather simple.

Women themselves mostly do not like to wear or collect used watches (but will certainly be exited to get a new one), unlike male collectors, who often wouldn't even mind if the watch was put aside during an exhumation if it's a model they always wanted.

'Small is beautiful!' Especially during the 1940s and into the 1950s, watches had been made extremely small. The gents' watches came smaller than today's ladies' watches. And the latter, at the time, were made extremely tiny, with a dial hard to read from a normal distance; it looks really odd if a man is wearing such a vintage gents' watch today. There are frequent discussions amongst collectors whether a specific timepiece from that period was really made for a male wearer.

Dedications, usually engraved on the back of the watch, can be interesting, especially when identifying the watch, but can also be a reason not to buy a vintage piece or at a substantially reduced price at best. *'To John Doe for 25 years of loyal service in the bookkeeping department'* is something many people shy away from, unless it's their uncle.

Other collectors avoid watches with intimate inscriptions such as *'to my beloved husband'* or *'to daddy from his children'*, but would make an exception with something like *'to Elvis from Priscilla'*.

It's also another thing if you have dedications in relation to history, our heroes in the military or *'to John Glenn – NASA 1962'*. Also more acceptable, a neutral inscription like: *'for 100.000 Kilometers Volkswagen 1965'*.

And there are other markings, scratched into the inside of the back lids by watchmakers, that dreadful habit of leaving their service- or repair marks no-one else understands. That might be marginally of interest in an old antique watch if it also indicates a date, otherwise it's just annoying. There are many interpretations what these codes mean or have meant in the past, but mostly only the individual watchmaker could cross-reference things to his ledger.

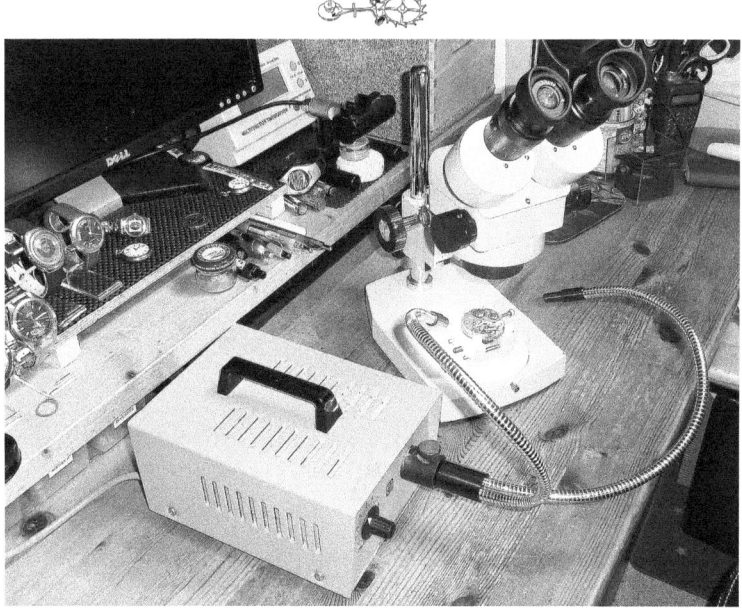

Above: stereo zoom microscope with a continuously zoomable magnification range, 3 to 45 times – ideal in the area of watchmaking and -servicing, with enough space available to work on the watch and a separate, effectively dimmable cold-light illumination. Of course, in practical application and not just for making an image for this book, the arms with the LEDs lights would have to come from the back. Identification of marks, checking escapements or hairsprings, etc. is made a lot easier, supplemental to the use of different loupes. Also high-resolution images can be taken with special cameras replacing one of the oculars.

All together a Rolex-watch value, but *'persistence spells success'* when looking for affordable, used equipment.

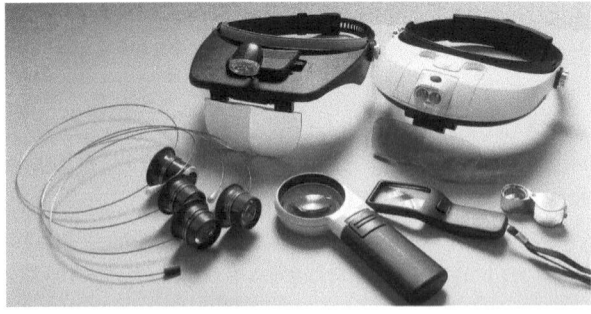

Different loupes and head loupes. They are more a tool for the workshop, but can also be helpful for a collector in many respects (with a perhaps limited number of them).

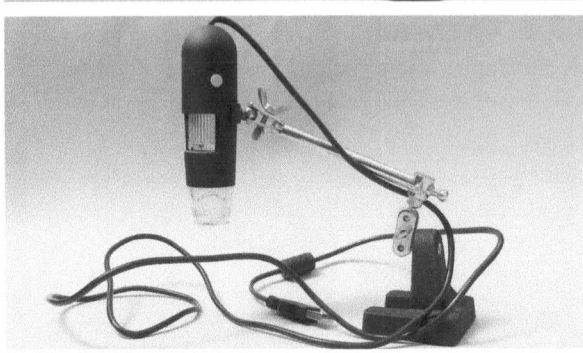

USB microscope, very useful when identifying numbers and markings or taking macro-images. For most applications, it's good enough to get a cheap version. If you should happen to be amongst the lucky 2.5% of the population, knowing how to operate them, perhaps with a new (self-made) stand, you will, with some knowledge about optical principles, not be one of the 97.5%, making them one of the most returned items by clueless contemporaries on Internet sales platforms.

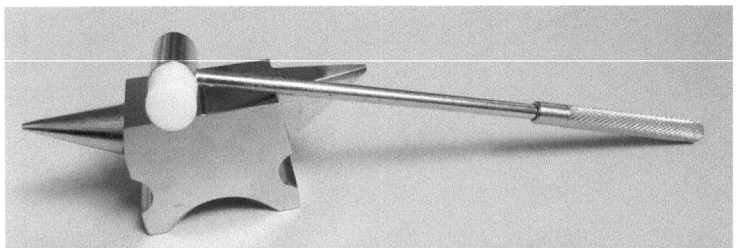

And if I had a hammer... A watchmaker's hammer is an often-used tool. It is much better to hold the pin pusher straight when working on a metal wristband and give it a little tap with the hammer, rather than wildly pushing around. Believe it or not. Professional watchmakers also use this hammer to set hands on a watch – very, very cautiously – already at the factory assembly process. Also here, you can hold the hand setting tool very straight, rather than pushing it by hand at a possible angle. Much better than using tweezers or a screwdriver to push things down (a preferred working approach of many 'pocket watch restorers'), often leaving bent hands and scratch marks.

WATCHES AND TIME

The authors of this book are neither watchmakers, nor special experts, just dedicated collectors, but in order to make things better understandable, there should be a general, short introduction to watches and time and the theories behind. This can naturally only contain a small and very rudimentary overview of the many topics which are of interest in this respect, without any claim to professional or scientific quality, especially as this book is more oriented towards collecting (or not). This might contain (hopefully not too many) mistakes or some unclear descriptions which the readers are forehand asked to excuse.

Dealing with a matter so complex, one will never find a single book or document giving a complete overview and information must be collected from different sources, but without ever coming to an end. Even a watchmaker, trained and working in his job for years, will always come across something new.

For someone with just an unspecific interest in watches and clocks, it is enough to seek some general information, perhaps a bit more about one or the other watch in possession and to be fascinated every now and then when coming across some items of interest within the art of watchmaking. Occasionally, it's even better to look at things like children, to enjoy a beautiful facade and to keep the spirit of fascination. Knowledge and insight also bring along a critical and questioning attitude, often spoiling the fun.

Very specific subjects have only briefly been touched; they could otherwise fill a book of their own.

Since thousands of years, man has undertaken great efforts to display time or measure time intervals. The course of the stars and the interaction between Mother Earth, the sun and the moon, had once been the sole source of orientation, based on astronomical observations and relying on the predictable nature of the movement of heavenly bodies. The existence of day and night and the time in between or the cycles of the ever-recurring seasons were easy to observe. But soon, this was not enough anymore.

It all started with the sundial, actually just a pole pushed into the ground, indicating the time with its moving shadow thrown by the sun. In addition, many timekeepers for short intervals have been created, for instance the hourglass, still today very popular in the kitchen or the water clock, measuring time by the amount of a regulated flow of water into or out from a vessel (inflow type or outflow type).

Many other constructions came up around the world, like in China, where a filament burns down in a jade bowl during the night and from which one could roughly evaluate the time elapsed.

The farmer orientated himself on the sunrise and sunset or the weather; otherwise, things took as long as needed.

The technical development of clocks and watches was an ongoing refining process, up to a mechanism, which is constantly driven by an internal force. This energy came at first from weights and later through a mainspring. In recent times, electricity is supplying the power coming from a small button cell.

Interlocking wheels and pinions in the gear train are ultimately moving the hands which indicate the time on a dial. The watchmakers use a special formula to give every wheel and pinon the right number of teeth to come to a correct reduction.

The force has to be controlled and regulated by an escapement. The first variant of such a mechanical-clock escapement was the 'foliot', a primitive type of balance, a horizontal bar with adjustable weights on the end. The power comes from a weight, also moving the clock's hands. The tension of the weight causes a drum wheel to rotate, which is itself turning an escape wheel (verge) preventing a free und uncontrolled rotation.

These early clocks had been highly inaccurate. Later clocks kept the verge escapement, but timekeeping came from a freely swinging pendulum, which substantially increased accuracy.

Pendulum clocks – meanwhile equipped with a better type escapement – and especially the regulators (very precise pendulum clocks) are still today very accurately running timekeepers. Compared to the requirements of past times, they had been sufficient in their precision, but need a fixed position whilst in operation. One could carry such watches around to other stable places, but they were not usable in a sensible manner during a trip.

Contrary to a pendulum mechanism, with weights delivering the power, the modern escapements are fairly independent from any movements of the watch or clock. This was made possible through the use of a mainspring as power source and a balance, mounted on an axle and held in oscillations by a spiral spring – the new clock generator. It functions like a circular pendulum with a special lever, which stops and releases the gear train in the pulse-beat of a pendulum, thereby portioning the energy.

A mechanical watch, on the whole and up to a certain stage, always shows the time correctly, despite decreasing strength of the mainspring. This is based on the physical property of a pendulum, called 'isochronism', deriving from the Greek word 'chronos' (time, also the God of time) and isos (equal, lasting the same time). Pendulums of the same length are always swinging at equal time intervals, independent from the distance of their travel.

This also functions in the construction of a balance with a spiral spring, whose fading amplitude (half of a full swing), in line with the decreasing power, does not change much in terms of duration. In practice, a perfect isochronal movement of a watch is of course only reached by top models, where also several imperfections and external influences are compensated.

Once, there was a special problem related to navigation at sea. Without the exact time, one could indeed determine the latitude, but not the longitude, at least not exact enough.

With only the latitude well know, ships were following a straight line along a constant latitude, called 'running down a westing' (or easting), preventing the ships from taking the most direct route or taking advantage of better winds and currents, which could save days or even weeks. Dangers of short rations, causing health problems of even death amongst the crew, had been permanent and navigational errors resulted in many shipwrecks.

When this problem was finally solved in the first half of the 18th century, it was a giant step forward and one of the most important achievements of mankind. Also, the decline of piracy at sea can, at least partly, be attributed to the fact that ships could now sail along other and more individual routes, also better calculable and controllable.

John Harrison (1693-1776), self-educated English carpenter and clockmaker, had invented the first marine chronometer and revolutionized navigation and safety of long-distance sea travel.

Before, a reward was offered by the British Parliament in the year 1714 to develop such a timepiece under the 'Longitude Act'. Harrison's watches are known as the H1, H2, H3 and H4 (the first Sea Watch).

He began working on a second Sea Watch, the H5, while testing of the H4 took place. As he felt that he was not treated well by the deciding committee, he was seeking the aid of King Georg III. and had at least received some of his rightful remunerations.

Later, the K1, an exact copy of the H4, was constructed by Larcum Kendall and used by Captain Cook on his second and third voyage around the world, whilst on the first trip, he was still relying on the lunar-distance-method. Cook was full of praise about the watch and the charts of the Southern Pacific Ocean he was able to make with the use of the K1, were remarkably accurate. The watch is today kept in the Royal Observatory, Greenwich at the National Maritime Museum, Greenwich.

The successor, the K2, was on a very special trip, famous around the world. It accompanied Lieutenant William Bligh, commander of HMS Bounty and was retained by Fletcher Christian (no, not Marlon Brando!), following the 'Mutiny on the Bounty'.

In 1840, it was brought back from Pitcairn Island, at the time the hiding place of the mutineers. It passed through several hands and is now kept in the National Maritime Museum in London.

Kendall wanted to further simplify the design and, above all, wanted to make it cheaper. The K1 had a price tag of 450 Pounds. The H4, the first successful sea chronometer, cost 400 Pounds in the year 1750, about one third of the price of a ship. The K3, his last watch, cost 100 Pounds, but did not have the required accuracy. The K3 is also kept in the Royal Observatory, Greenwich, like the H1, H2, H3 and the H4.

The latter H4, mother of all marine chronometers, is left in a stopped state, because unlike the first three, it requires oil for lubrication, which will degrade as it runs. *'Why don't they frequently oil it?'* you might say. Well, it's really a large pocket watch and would need each time a complete disassembly for that.

The H5 is today owned by the Worshipful Company of Clockmakers in London.

At some stage, people wanted to carry around time also privately, at first as small portable clocks, then as pocket- and lastly as wristwatches. However, when the first modern clocks and watches became available, individual timekeeping for the masses, outside the circles of privileged people, did not exist for a long time, actually not until the beginning of the Industrial Age.

Then, the automatic watches came along (bumper- and later the rotor types), which made a manual winding-up superfluous. This was now, when worn, simply effected through the movement of the wrist.

The type of the escapements changed over the years, from the verge escapement in early pocket watches, to different types of lever escapements or the cheaper cylinder escapement. The typical Swiss lever escapement, as shown on the front cover page top right (with the basics invented by Ferdinand Adolf Lange, Glashuette, Germany) has however remained the measure of all things in mechanical timepieces.

Different variants of regulation, better bearing of the shafts, technical innovations as well as inventions relating to the balance and balance wheel itself, have helped to improve the precision and reliability of the mechanical watches, even in later times, when they have long lost the race for precision against the quartz watches.

The next step forward came with the idea to put a battery (button cell) into the watch, powering an electric motor and replacing the driving force that formerly came from a mainspring. The electric watch was born, but at first, everything else was still mechanical. The electric components (movable components, like switches and magnets) were later replaced by electronic components (solid-state, transistors and diodes), facilitating the introduction of the electronic watches.

The escapement, provider of the regulated oscillations and clocking of the gear train, was the next thing which came into focus with the aim to increase the frequency of oscillations and thus the accuracy of the watch. At the same time, the number of moving parts has steadily been reduced.

With the electricity now inside the watch, other use could be made besides just driving a motor. The tuning fork watch was developed, where a device, similar to a tuning fork, provides the oscillating frequencies for regulation, typically 300, 360 or 720 Hertz, occasionally also something in between (compared to 2.5 to 5.0 Hertz of the existing mechanical and semi-mechanical watches).

For the musicians amongst the readers: the concert pitch 'A' has a frequency of 440 Hertz. You can hear the humming sound of the tuning fork inside if you hold the watch to the ear.

The technique was developed by Max Hetzel, at the time an employee of Bulova. The originals, the Bulova Accutrons, are *'humming'* at 360 Hertz.

The tuning forks were then replaced by a quartz crystal. Due to the properties of the quartz, it will oscillate at a perfectly high frequency (normally at 32,768 Hertz) when electric current runs through. The watches became extremely accurate at this stage, within seconds a month. The first quartz watch was built by Warren Marrison and J.W. Horton at Bell Telephone Laboratories, but only the advent of solid-state electronic components had allowed making them small and inexpensive.

The battery sends its electricity to the quartz crystal trough an electronic circuit. The quartz starts to oscillate back and forth. The circuit, based on the number of vibrations and their electronic reduction, generates electric impulses, one per second. They either power and control a LCD-display or drive a small motor (stepper motor), turning the wheels in the gear train that spin the second-, minute- and hour hand of an analogue display.

The quartz, as an impulse generator, was temporarily implemented also in semi-mechanical watches, as the pure quartz technology came along, namely in the tuning fork- and also in the electronic watches, without changing the basics of their mechanical elements:

1. The tuning-fork watches with the Bulova movement caliber 224 inside are regulated by a quartz crystal. The active tuning fork became a passive element then, vibrating under the control of a quartz oscillator.

2. The Q Quartz by Timex, which was also only shortly produced before they started to make normal quartz watches, was simply a quickly created interim-solution by putting an electronic oscillator, regulated by a quartz crystal, on top of an electric/electronic-mechanical movement.

And finally (if you ignore the latest Smartwatches as a genuine horological product), the radio-controlled watches marked the end of the technical development outside scientific applications. They are normal quartz watches with an important exception: they are receiving signals from an atomic clock, frequently sent out and adjusting these watches if necessary.

They also get the data for the date, weekday and month, year, the additional day in a leap year, the leap second when time is adjusted to the slowing down of the Earth's rotation and the switch between standard time (winter time) and summer time (daylight savings time). If they are also solar powered, with no more battery necessary, we are at the end of the line of watchmaking and time keeping. If the radio-controlled watch is outside the reach of the radio signals, it runs on as a normal quartz watch.

Junghans, Germany, came out with the first radio-controlled wristwatch in 1990, the MEGA1 (two models shown in the book on page 103). The large antenna was still integrated in the wristband, which was not so practical, and replacements of the band were (are) expensive, but the reception of the radio waves is exceptionally good.

Later, the antennas, now smaller and more compact, went inside the case in the form of a miniature ferrite rod antenna. Wristbands could now be changed like on a normal watch.

Before that, Junghans came to the market in 1985 with this technique in various types of clocks.

The digitally coded time transfer for radio-controlled clocks was invented by Wolfgang Hilberg, working at the time for Telefunken, Germany. He filed a patent in 1967. Initially, nobody wanted to produce such a radio-controlled wristwatch, and the boom only began after the patent for Wolfgang Hilberg had run out.

An atomic clock with that kind of precision cannot be constructed as a small, portable version, but only as a larger installation in a scientific institution. An atomic clock can show the absolutely precise time. Any micro-deviations are totally insignificant in normal use. We would have to wait several million years to have a possible nonconformity of +/- 1 second.

Well, it needs to be mentioned that there is indeed an atomic clock, somewhat limited, for the wrist. The Bathys Cesium 133 is the first true atomic wristwatch. It has an accuracy of 'only' +/- 1 second in 1,000 years. If that is no obstacle for you and if you accept that it runs only 36 hours after the battery is charged, your frantic search for total independence in accurate timekeeping might be worth spending a few thousand dollars here, instead of getting yourself an expensive mechanical luxury watch, after all quite inferior in accuracy.

The precision of the atomic clocks has steadily improved up to a maximum deviation of +/- 1 second in 40, 50 or 150 million years and coming ever closer to 1 billion years. In continuous operation, a maximum deviation of +/- 1 second in 730 million years has already been reached. That is equal to the time needed by light to travel 30 centimeters. In short term operation, that precision has even been superseded.

There is no simple quartz crystal 'swinging' in the atomic clocks. The timing is derived from the characteristic frequency of radiative transition of the electrons orbiting an atom's nucleus, 'jumping' back and forth between energy states. The length of one second is equal to 9,192,631,770 cycles of the radiation that gets an atom of the element cesium to vibrate between two energy states = 9,192,631,770 Hertz (full cycles per second).

To sum up the various stages of development, we have the following types of watches:

- **Mechanical watch**
- **Electric watch**
- **Electronic watch**
- **Tuning fork watch**
- **Quartz controlled electric/electronic watch**
- **Quartz controlled tuning fork watch**
- **Quartz watch**
- **Quartz watch/radio controlled by an atomic clock**
- and, presently still something exotic, the **atomic wristwatch.**

Above: not only for the workshop, but also nice to have for the collector: The left device is used for testing and loosening quartz watch wheel trains without opening the watch, perhaps on that *'not running, just needs batteries'* -watch you just purchased. With the instrument on the right, you can test the motor and the battery, also without opening the watch. It has a simple battery tester to check the condition of a button cell before you use it.

Above: ultrasonic cleaning device. When cleaning cases of old pocket watches, you come across more or less dirty or oxidized surfaces, but they have mostly been kept in the pocket when carried around. It is something different when doing a thorough cleansing of a used wristwatch. We should leave aside mentioning used leather wristbands straight away, occasionally requiring some overcoming to get through with the yucky stuff. But even metal bracelets and cases have a lot of places for gunk to hide. No wonder that nurses are not allowed to wear a watch on the wrist in sensible areas.

If you have done this kind of cleaning work for a number of times, you should be well prepared for the job of a crime scene cleaner or to work for the local sewer rehabilitation company.

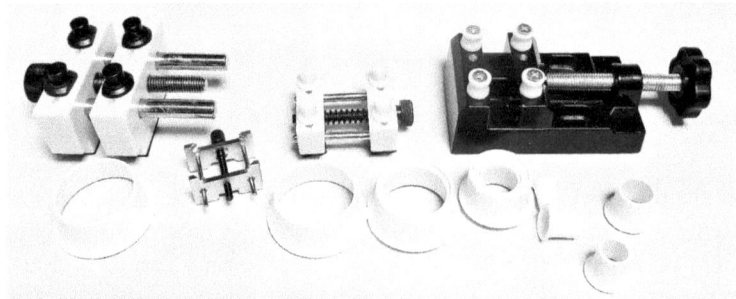

Above: different movement holders to securely hold and protect the watch or movement when working on it.

THE QUARTZ CRISIS AND THE REVIVAL OF THE MECHANICAL WATCHES

Providing the time for Tom, Dick and Harry has become worthless under a commercial point of view, they get it for free. He, who knows what time it is or shows it on a non-watch product, gets no money for it anymore. But then, why do prices go up for mechanical watches?

The upcoming of the quartz watches marked the end for many manufacturers of mechanical watches. The markets had been flooded with cheap quartz watches, especially from the Far East, which were not only cheaper to produce, but also much more precise and did not need a frequent winding. Finally, the conventional dial and the hands for hours, minutes and seconds could be replaced by LED and LCD indications (LED = light emitting diode, LCD = liquid crystal display). With those, the number of moving parts was practically brought to zero (leaving aside pushers for setting the watch). Nevertheless, most of the quartz watches today came back to the familiar analogue display.

The quartz watches dominate within the mass of products, but only by their sheer number and not so distinct within the monetary value of the annual turnover and certainly not in the collector's markets, notwithstanding the fact, that you can also find rather expensive quartz watches from prime manufacturers.

The world market for watches is dominated by just a few countries. Switzerland and China are ahead. Other important watchmaking countries are Hong Kong (if you want to treat it separately), Germany, France, Singapore, Italy, Japan or Great Britain. Looking at the value of the individual watches, China leads by number of watches produced, but these are typically in the lowest price sector and mostly quartz watches, down to a sales price of US $1.99. The even make fake 'chronographs' in China which have no function in this respect, with dummy stop- and set buttons and sub dials with non-movable hands, acting just as decorations – *disgusting!*

In the upper- and luxury price segments (almost exclusively mechanical watches), Switzerland is by far the world leader. With just 2.5% share of individual pieces produced globally, the three biggest watchmaking groups of Switzerland alone account for 30% to 50% in terms of worldwide total turnover in monetary value. The statistics naturally vary from year to year.

Interesting to know: About half of all highly priced Swiss watches are bought by the Chinese – after all, they are number 5 in the ranking of the oldest civilizations on Earth, with some wear and tear of ethical standards in recent times, when it comes to make genuine products of their own.

But comparisons by country, especially involving China, naturally gives a strongly distorted picture. With almost 1.4 billion people, China must obviously lead every statistic, be it the number of people picking their nose or wearing brown shoes.

Admittedly, Swiss watchmaking and its history are something stunningly impressive, but if you take a close look about what's inside a watch, you will be surprised where many of that came from.

The list of some inventions by British watchmakers is undoubtedly remarkable: Robert Hooke, balance spring (1664), Daniel Quare, minute hand (1690), Henry Sully, oil sink (1715), Jahn Harrison, temperature compensation (1753), Thomas Mudge, lever escapement (1755), John Whitehurst, center seconds (1765), Thomas Young, chronograph (1807), Thomas Prest, keyless winding (1820), John Harwood, automatic winding (1924).

Of course, many other countries have contributed to the development of the industry, which often disappears behind the curtain of time.

The Germans are generally regarded as the first makers of portable watches, or better clocks small enough to be carried around, but lately, the question comes up about who really made the first portable watch, Peter Henlein (1479 – 1542) from Nuremberg, Germany, or someone else. Scientists today believe that this was already an ongoing process before the early 16th century.

Many German watchmaking companies were located in an area that became the 'DDR' after the war. Joining the existing enterprises in the West again, after the re-unification, many came back to old glory and the upper segment, when the companies came under control of new investors with the aim to continue old traditions and standards.

Watchmakers in the former East had been nationalized under Soviet control and working in horological kolkhozes, producing for the DDR itself, as well as the COMECON states, at whatever quality, and supplying the West with cheaper (nevertheless reliable) products against hard currency.

Collectors have to be careful when seeking to buy watches from certain companies and must clearly distinguish between three periods: pre-war – time in the former DDR – and after the reunification and reorientation out of the 'socialistic mishmash', which sometimes makes it difficult to sort things out.

The miraculous revival of the mechanical watches is a trend that still continues amongst the lovers and collectors of watches. And all that against the competition of much cheaper to produce and more accurate quartz watches.

Mechanical timepieces, especially those of highest quality (new or vintage collector's items), are more than ever thought-after. This is all happening in a period in which time, as a commercial product, has generally become worthless, aside from special applications.

Microwave ovens, TV sets, recorders, heating regulators, shutter controls, computers, smartphones, etc. can show us also the time; they need it for their own operations and as an additional information, you get it for free.

Showing the right time is obviously not everything; to some it is more important *what* is showing the time. Continuous efforts are made to technically improve mechanical watches and their preciseness. It's the race of the stage coaches against the trains, but with higher value and more exclusiveness of the mechanical timepieces.

Le Locle, Switzerland, postcard image from 1907. The city is known as the center of Swiss watchmaking and even cited as the birthplace of the industry, with roots dating back to the 1600s. The watchmaking, as an industry, was brought to Le Locle in the 17th century by Daniel Jeanrichard, who encouraged farmers of the area to make watch components for him during the long winters. Le Locle and the neighboring town La Chaux-de-Fonds, both mono-industrial watch manufacturing towns, have received recognition by the UNESCO in 2009 as world heritage sites for their unique architecture. The cityscape reflects the dominance of the watchmaking industry, with a unique scheme of parallel strips of intermingling residential houses and workshops.

RADIUM CONTAMINATION

Left: professional Geiger counter. This instrument comes from military inventory with an especially large and highly sensitive probe. It reliably picks up alpha-, beta- and gamma radiations. Good for checking radioactive material on dial and hands. The watch itself might not be 'glowing' anymore, but especially the radium is still there on older watches, with a half-life of 1600 (!) years. The radium itself is not glowing and is just an activator for the luminous material. The more harmless tritium had replaced the radium, and lately unhazardous materials are used. Many watchmakers today are refusing to work on certain vintage watches or are very reluctant in this respect. Today, non-radioactive material is the standard.

Left: the 'Radium-Girls': workers at the US Radium Corporation, New Jersey, USA. The company was mainly active in the extraction of radium from carnotite ore for the production of luminous paint and was a major supplier to the military in WWI and years beyond. Mostly women were painting radium lumed watches and instruments. The dangers of radium had not really been understood in these days and many of these women died due to radium contamination. Radium is especially dangerous when it gets *inside* the body – a thing to remember when working on such watches, as this stuff, often detached from the dial and hands, might get onto the workbench and via the fingers into the body with the next Pizza (also via inhaling radioactive dust particles). The way the radium got inside the bodies of these workers was ingestion, as many of them used their mouth to form a tip on the radium tainted paintbrushes. Some, in total unawareness of the problem, even painted their fingernails or teeth for fun with the deadly paint. What most people or watch collectors don't know: there are country-specific regulations concerning the shipment, storage and disposal of items containing radioactive substances, which also includes watch parts of that type.

CLOCKING OF WATCHES, CORRESPONDING AMPLITUDES

The regulation of the movement of a watch, which is driven by weights or a mainspring, needs an escapement. This is a component consisting of an escape wheel and escape lever, with a balance wheel for timing. There are two things which are important, the rate (frequency) of the oscillation – the higher, the better – and the accuracy of keeping this frequency.

At first, a pendulum was setting the beat. That all had already been discovered by Galileo Galilei around the year 1640, including the phenomena of isochronism (pendulums of the same length always need the same time to swing back and forth, independent from their distance of travel). The adjustment of the pendulum is done by changing its length. It triggers an action of the movement with every passage on its way. Galileo Galilei's son Vincenzo has later pursued this in practice. Around the same time, Christian Huygens, a Dutch mathematician and scientist from Le Hague, occupied himself with the construction of a watch regulated by a pendulum.

Pendulum clocks run very precise, especially if the influence on the length of the pendulum (shrinking, expansion), triggered by temperature changes, can be avoided or limited. This can for instance be achieved by a wooden pendulum rod, instead of a metal version.

Although the pendulums are swinging at the lowest rate compared to all other regulations, the timing is held well under control, because they can keep their rhythm very constant. There is, however, a serious drawback: they are excellent timekeepers, but not particularly good transportable and usable only in a vibration-free state.

The escapement with the swinging balance wheel and the spiral spring, as we know them in mechanical watches today, has subsequently replaced the pendulum. It is still in use today, in principle unchanged, with some technical enhancements which do not alter the basics. The frequencies have been improved and in parallel their steadiness.

Oscillation, beats, vibrations, amplitude, cycles, and swings: These are terms which are often used in a confusing and misleading fashion. If we take a pendulum (the balance wheel works alike): an oscillation, full swing, full beat, full cycle is the way from one turning point to the other, and back (A-B-A). An amplitude, vibration, half beat, half-cycle, half-oscillation, half-swing, goes just from one side to the other (A-B or B-A).

The timing by the balance is defined and constructed in amplitudes (half-oscillations) per hour (A/h), formulated for instance as $f = 18{,}000$ A/h.

The duration of a pendulum's (half-) swing depends on its length. The so-called seconds-pendulum needs one second for a half-swing (3,600 A/h). The length needed to achieve this is about 99.4 centimeters.

Due to different gravity effects in different places on Earth, this varies between 99.1 and 99.6 centimeters. Most clocks, down to the table clocks, have smaller pendulums. These are swinging faster and the mechanism and the ratio of gearing behind has to be structured accordingly.

To make a pendulum swing twice as fast (half-seconds pendulum), its length of 99.4cm must not be divided by 2, but by 4, resulting in a pendulum of approximately 24.9cm.

To make it swing three times as fast, the length of 99.4cm would not be divided by 3, but by 9, resulting in a pendulum of approximately 11cm.

Vice versa, in order to halve the speed (1,800 A/h), the length would not have to be doubled, but quadrupled.

The big wall clocks with a seconds-pendulum (length approximately 99.4 cm) have 3,600 half-beats per hour = 60 per minute = 1 second for a half-beat = 1 full cycle every 2 seconds = 0.5 Hertz.

Old pocket watches are ticking with 12,600 half-beats per hour (12,600 A/h) = 3.5 beats per second / 1.75 full oscillations per second. Very soon this has changed and 18,000 A/h became the standard = 5 half beats per second / 2.5 full oscillations per second, which is also the basis for the normal wristwatch. This went up, especially in wristwatches, to 21,600 A/h = 6 half-beats per second / 3 full oscillations per second.

Then came the high-speed oscillators in better movements, with 25,200 A/h = 7 half-beats per second / 3.5 full oscillations per second, 28,800 A/h = 8 half-beats per second / 4 full oscillations per second, up to 36,000 A/h = 10 half-beats per second / 5 full oscillations per second. The development has basically stopped here; some manufacturers even went back, as these high frequencies caused certain problems concerning bearings or lubrication for example. There are some exceptions still going further towards even higher beats (Super High Beat) in mechanical watches, but there are too special and can be left aside here.

To make the amplitudes better comparable, the regulating frequency of mechanical watches must be converted into Hertz, the standard for the modern watches, from the tuning fork- the quartz regulated watches, up to the atomic clocks.

The official formula: f = A/h : (2 x 3600). For instance, 18.000 : 7200 = 2.5 (example for a watch swinging at 18,000 A/h)

Making things more simple: **The Hertz rate equals the number of oscillations (full swings, two amplitudes) per second.**

32

Example: an amplitude of 18,000 A/h equals 9,000 oscillations (full swings) per hour, 150 oscillations per minute, 2.5 oscillations per second = 2.5 Hertz.

With the tuning fork watches, the frequencies went up considerably. They are *'humming'* at a frequency of 300, 360 and up to 720 Hertz.

The quartz watches finally brought the quantum leap. Not only can they be produced much cheaper, they are at the same time much more precise.

The quartz is designed to swing at a frequency of 32,768 Hertz. This frequency was arbitrarily standardized at 32,768 Hertz, but a power of 2 had to be chosen (here: 2 by the power of 15 = 32,768), so that a simple chain of digital divided-by-2-stages can backwards produce the 1 Hz signal (one impulse per second) needed to drive the watch's second hand, whose driving wheel is connected through the gear train with the wheels moving the other hands. The impulse is sent to a stepper motor, but can also go to a counter module and then show the time on a digital display.

32.768 oscillations, divided backwards, allow 15 flip-flops (electronic second-impulses, based on frequency divisions by 2). The flip-flop is a basic and indispensable element of the digital technique. A pulse at input flips an electronic switch into one of two stable states and stays there until a second impulse will flop it back into its previous state.

Typical quartz watches have a precision of +/- 10 to 20 seconds per month or better in high accuracy quartz movements. The latter can for instance measure temperature and adjust for it.

Any deviations are constant, if not subject to external or other influences. In this sense, a quartz watch runs always precise (even if slow or fast), as any deviations accumulate (up or down) in a steady rate.

Even the most accurate quartz watches need an occasional re-setting, but naturally less often than a mechanical watch whose deviations are furthermore fluctuating.

Recently, UHF/ultra-high frequency quartz watches came along, made by Bulova, with a beat rate of 262,144 Hertz (2 by the power of 18), perhaps in competition against the radio-controlled wristwatches, although the precision of a regular quartz watch ought to be good enough for everyday use.

Bulova engineers were often moving ahead, like with the tuning fork watches (Accutron) or the quartz controlled tuning forks (Accuquartz).

Atomic clocks (cesium based), which can also send their signal to radio-controlled watches, have a frequency of over 9 billion Hertz or precisely 9,192,631,770 Hertz (oscillations per second).

A comparison of various types follows on the next page.

Type of clock/watch	Amplitude/Hertz
One-second pendulum – 3,600 A/h	0.5
Half-second pendulum – 7,200 A/h	1.0
Quarter-second pendulum – 10,800 A/h	1.5
Pocket watch / wristwatch – 18,000 A/h	2.5
Wristwatch – 21,600 A/h	3.0
Wristwatch – 25,200 A/h	3.5
Wristwatch – 36,000 A/h	5.0
Tuning Fork Watches	300 to 720
Quartz Watch	32,768
High Beat Quartz Watch	262,144
Cesium Atomic Clock (also regulating radio-controlled watches)	9,192,631,770

One can easily see that the quartz watches are controlled by substantially higher frequencies than mechanical watches, by a significant factor of about 10,000, depending on the compared mechanical model – a quantum leap. The latter, no matter how expensive they are, can never be so precise.

With the radio-controlled watch, receiving radio signals from an atomic clock, deviations are reduced to +/- 1 second in several million years.

Above left: Constructional drawing of a pendulum clock by Galileo Galilei, which he designed around 1640. The project was later realized in practice by his son Vincenzo. **Above right:** Galileo Galilei

Let's come back in more detail on the issue of the amplitude of a watch. It is important in relation to its performance; some even call it the most important factor. It is something we need if we want to know more about the condition of a particular watch, especially the movement. This can be tested with a device called timegrapher (as shown on the next page), along with other elements like the beat error (irregularities between 'tick and tack') or the deviation from accuracy, expressed in seconds per day.

The amplitude, which is often called the 'heart beat' of a watch, is an element of distance *within* the time of a swing. The duration (time) of a swing, as we have learned from Galileo Galilei, is equal on all pendulums of the same length (and accordingly on balance wheels), independent from their distance of travel (isochronism); in other words, pendulums of the same length travelling a longer way are moving faster, and the ones making a shorter distance are moving slower. High amplitude means a longer (distance-wise!), but faster travel and makes the watch more precise. Remember: The duration remains the same.

What makes people usually confused, are the numbers referring to a good amplitude. Let's just take 250°. Some might be tempted to add this up to 500°, but a full turn of a wheel means 360°. How can that be?

Well, these are two separate movements. When thinking of specific drawings of oscillations, also in other areas, with waves over and below a line in the middle which they are crossing (this is also the right graphic depiction for the amplitudes of a watch), imagine the movements from the middle to one side and back and from the middle to the other side and back. The swing of a pendulum could be seen in the same way, with its starting point straightly perpendicular = point 0, with A and B as the high points to the sides. An amplitude (half oscillation) would then be 0-A-0 or 0-B-0 and a full oscillation 0-A-0-B-0.

It would not make sense to go into more technical detail here, as we are talking about collecting watches and not constructing, but we can note, that the amplitude is limited anyway somewhere in the vicinity of 320° (each half swing), due to constructional obstacles.

High amplitudes of prime watches are typically in the range of 270° to 315° if the watch is fully wound, going down to perhaps 220° to 260° with half the power left.

Thanks to the physical laws of isochronism, a watch can run fairly well with 180° amplitude, under the appreciation that we are dealing with a – possibly un-serviced – vintage watch. It does the job, if only occasionally worn and if you are not responsible for timely starts of rocket launches at Cape Canaveral.

And don't worry when you read about impressive numbers published by manufacturers of luxury watches, making you feel that anything below 290° is of inferior quality.

Always keep in mind that any precise checking of the amplitude on the timegrapher requires a lift-angle to be known (a geometric feature of the movement). The 52° set as default are usually identical or close enough to the actual lift angle of the watch, which will eventually produce acceptable results only marginally away from the correct figure.

However, there can be larger variations with watches having a lift angle much different from this default setting (e.g. the Omega pocket watch on page 135).

Indispensable: a timegrapher for analyzing watches and to make adjustments or to get the necessary feedback for jobs to be done. It shows the deviation in secs/day, the amplitude, the beat-error in m/s and the beat number (A/h). The microphone is rotatable in the horizontal and vertical level, to make tests in different positions of the watch.

On test here: a vintage watch after coming back from service and repair, with best results: an amplitude of 294°, a beat error (between tick and tack) of only 0.1 milliseconds, 18.000 A/h automatically detected. The +7 s/d (seven seconds fast per day) is left as it is; the watch behaves differently when worn on the wrist.

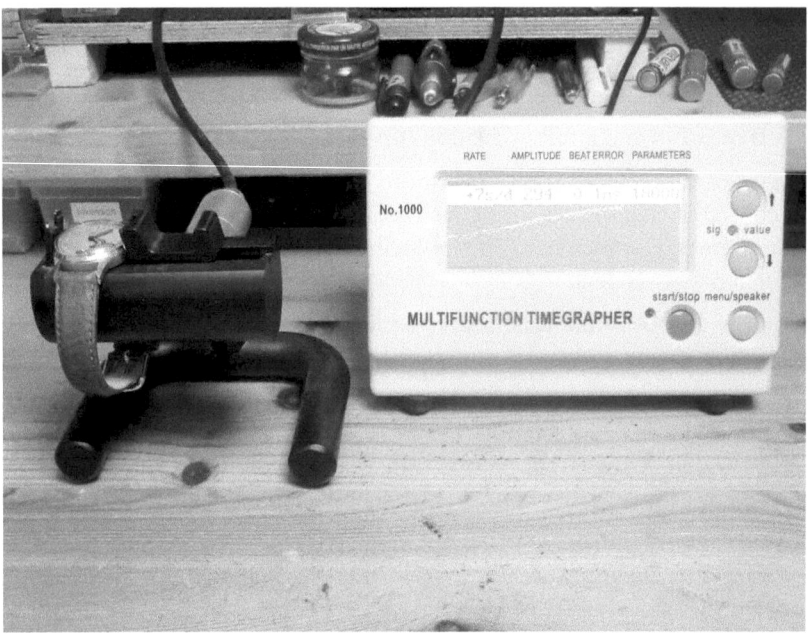

TIME – ONE OF THE STANDARD UNITS

Dealing with the theory of time, one will soon realize that things are much more complicated than expected.

Sooner or later, the need to come to reasonably standard units had emerged. This was not only becoming more and more important in every stage of technological development, but setting standards was also the precondition and driving force to reach the next level. Three things needed to be standardized at first (besides four others which came later): length, weight and time. The combination of distance and time gives us the speed.

Length: Within the metric system, the exact length of 1 meter has been defined and therefrom upwards, the kilometer = 1000 meters and downwards the decimeter = 1/10 of a meter, centimeter = 1/100 of a meter, millimeter = 1/1.000 of a meter, micrometer (micron/µm) = 1/1.000.000 (1 millionth) of a meter and nanometer = 1/1.000.000.000 (1 billionth) of a meter. The unit of microns is used to define the thickness of gold plating on watch cases or metal wristbands for example. People usually refer to a micron as a 1/1.000 of a millimeter rather than 1/1.000.000 of a meter, which would be more correct.

In 1794, the so-called geographical definition was used, defining a meter as 1/10,000,000 of the length the meridian quadrant going through Paris. There has been another approach to define what the length of a meter should be, with a second-pendulum of a watch as reference. It was known, that in order to swing from one side to the other (amplitude, half-beat), a pendulum needs certain length of about 99.1 to 99.6 centimeters, but due to different gravitational conditions around the world, this was not precise enough.

A gauge block was produced in 1799 as the archetype of a meter, a platinum-iridium bar measured in an ambient temperature at the melting point of ice. It is kept today in the International Bureau for Weights and Measurements in Paris and copies of it can be found in specific places around the world.

Time as a reference came back in the calculation of the length of a meter. They had to get away from the old prototype meter, which itself is subject to miniscule changes in its length and stretches and shrinks with the slightest changes of temperature. Since 1983 and until today, a meter is equal to the distance light travels in a vacuum in 1/299,792,458 seconds.

The combination of time and distance, now in absolute accuracy, has been the basis for other technical developments, like the GPS-system. The GPS-satellites are equipped with more than one atomic-clock (usually accurate to +/- 1 second in some 10,000 years). The precise time, together with the exact position of the satellite, is an important requirement for the accuracy of the positioning.

If we would measure signals from GPS satellites with a household wristwatch, one would try to find his way around in London and end up in Scotland (perhaps a bit exaggerated). Pilots landing at narrow strips at night, surveyors, prospectors and farmers with GPS-guided tractors, all appreciate a higher precision.

Weight: A weight is the result of the mass of a body which is attracted by the gravitation of the Earth. The kilo is not a unit of weight, but a unit of mass, equal to the prototype of the kilogram kept in Paris, a block of platinum-iridium. The pound is a weight, a unit of force.

Mass and weight are often confused with each other. As the gravitation on Earth is not equal everywhere, the weight is also not equal everywhere, but a mass is, even on the moon (where it will be 6 times lighter in weight).

According to the present norms, a liter of water, the old unit, weighs 0,998 kg. Earlier, the kilogram was defined as a decimeter (liter) of water at its highest density at 3.98°C under normal pressure.

People are puzzled lately over the problem that the prototype of the kilo in Paris is losing weight (50 micro-grams so far), as opposed to the many copies made. Now, the experts want to link the kilogram to a unit of measurement in quantum physics, the Planck constant. Using a thing called watt balance, scientists can relate the mass of the object to the electrical energy needed to move it.

This new definition would bring the kilogram (mass) in line with the six other base units that complete the International System of Units (SI), consisting of seven units, which are the meter (distance), the ampere (electric current), the mole (substance), the kelvin (temperature), the candela (luminosity) and the time (seconds). They all are now based on universal constants of nature; the kilogram was the last hold-out.

Time: Lots of complications with the other units, but what about time? Isn't it all a lot easier here, as days (consisting of day and night) and the seasons all return periodically and define the rhythm and length of the time-periods? One can simply apportion the day segments into hours, minutes and seconds. And the period over the four seasons, until returning to the beginning, is called a year, divided into months and days.

Leaving aside the fact, that day and night, within the course of the year, are not of constant length, this is exactly done this way, but this is not precise enough and subject to changes.

In the course of time, new discoveries have been made which have helped to refine the system, but they are also somewhat frightening, revealing the consequential impotence man is faced with, especially what concerns the phenomenon of time, no matter how exactly we can define and measure it.

The mysteries of space and time are something the physicists should better deal with and rack their brains what time really is. No wonder that many of them have also become philosophers.

Whatever, at least we can try to measure time with ever greater precision. But in the end and in its larger dimension, it's like counting money in a currency whose value we don't know. Everything is based on physical and chemical processes and systemic events in the infinitive width of the Universe. The Earth with its human beings is nothing but an insignificant part in the overall system and will someday cease to exist, with or without our influence.

Albert Einstein, especially concerned with physical theories of time, space and gravitation, was checking the time in normal life on his Longines wristwatch. It has been made in 1929 and was given to him in 1931 as a gift.

In the year 2005, it fetched a price of US $596.000 at an auction, the highest price ever paid for a Longines watch. This was, of course, also due to the prominent name of the former owner, but we frequently see even much higher prices paid on vintage watches, which are not connected to a special person. He also had a pocket watch of the same manufacturer, which is displayed today in the Historical Museum in Berne, Switzerland.

The Earth rotates around the sun within a year, and at the same time it is turning around its own axis, for which it needs 1 day. Man has divided a year into 365 days and 12 months of different length. The day consists of 24 hours, or 1.440 minutes or 86.400 seconds. We know that the Earth needs a bit longer than 365 days to complete a full circle around the sun, about one fourth of a day. This is why we have a leap year every 4 years with another day added in the month of February.

But what about the days and hours? Doesn't a day always have 24 hours, only with a different length of day and night within this time span?

No, that is not the case! Whilst the Earth steadily makes its orbit around the sun, the rotation around its own axis is not constant. This rotation progressively slows down overall. One day, which will certainly not be reached by mankind, at least here on Earth, it's closing time for our planet.

The situation at its final standstill has been described in many theories. But this is not so important, as all will be an ongoing process over millions of years, with dramatic consequences long before. It's also totally useless to demonstrate models of a *sudden* standstill (which will never be the case), when everything not attached to bedrock will continue to spin sideways around the Earth.

So, let's look at the final situation after a continuous slowdown, some 4 billion years away: all the water has flown towards the poles. A mega continent has been formed in the middle around the equator, between two oceans on the top and on the bottom, which have flooded everything else.

The super continent is uninhabitable in the middle, without water, and whatever is still crawling around on Earth (perhaps some insects) has moved to the north- and south coasts. A day would last as long as a year, with 6 months of day and night. During 'daytime', the temperature will rise to about 100° Celsius.

Whatever, if you have heard or read about other versions, varying from the before mentioned, the final result is always the same.

Enough of scary perspectives, but even still so far away from the inevitable end, we cannot totally ignore things. 370 million years ago, due to the faster rotation of the Earth around its own axis, a day had only 22 hours, based on today's length and definition of time, and the year had approx. 400 (shorter) days.

That has long been recognized. As we cannot periodically change the length of hours, minutes and seconds, an adjustment is occasionally made through a leap second, which is added to the running time. Thus, the overall time is synchronized to the slowing of the self-rotation of the Earth under retention of the existing standard time units.

Owners of radio-controlled watches don't notice this when the watch is corrected accordingly via radio signals. Too bad for the owner of an expensive mechanical luxury watch who, unknowingly, is checking its accuracy and compares it to a radio-controlled watch or clock, just during the very minute which is given an extra second.

61 seconds in relation to 60 means a second off per minute, 60 seconds per hour and 24 minutes per day – a disaster, and perhaps a wickedly expensive Patek Philippe Tourbillon is thrown away through the open window.

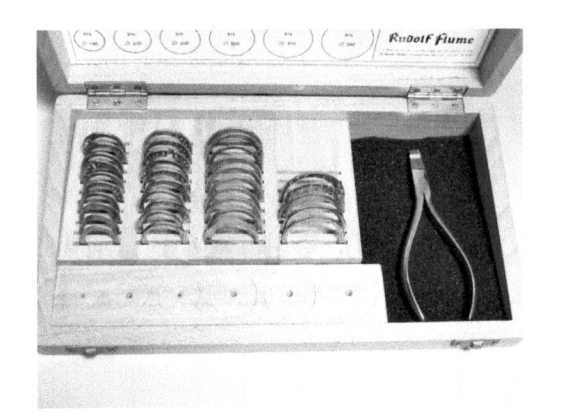

Above left: old toolset for lifting acrylic watch crystals by Flume, Germany. **Above right:** modern crystal lift by Bergeon, Switzerland.

MECHANICAL WRISTWATCHES, HAND WIND

As some people are getting occasionally confused: The mechanics inside (clockwork = fixed, moving parts and wheels) are called the **movement**. The clocking of the beat is done by a mechanical linkage called the **escapement**.

History tells us that the idea of wearing a watch differently came long before the modern wristwatches have been made, especially in the form of small watches on bracelets made for ladies. They were really more a piece of jewelry set with precious stones – beauty before function. Watches on the wrist were therefore considered to be not suitable for men – *'something for the ladies'* – too small, too delicate to be accurate timekeepers and too much at risk to be damaged. This has substantially curbed their ultimate development and introduction.

The use by the military around the time of WWI was the driving force, before general acceptance followed. Many claim to have invented the wristwatch, but there was really nothing to be invented; an existing product was just worn differently, at least in the beginning, when they still were smaller pocket watches, strapped to the wrist. For some time, the wristbands were not fixed on removable spring bars between the lugs, but attached to fixed brackets, soldered to the case. Later, they got their own typical cases and specially designed movements.

Above left: A step far back near to the early beginnings of modern wristwatches. **1919 OMEGA**, Swiss, movement Omega cal. 27.9 SIBN, enameled dial, gold plated Dennison Moon case (Dennison Watch Case Co., England), plating guaranteed for 20 years, Ø 30mm.

Above right: 1930s OMEGA, Swiss, gold plated Dennison Moon case (Dennison Watch Case Co., England), movement Omega cal. 26.5 SOB, Ø 30mm. The watch has the typical 'watchmaker's 4' on the dial, the Roman numeral IV written as IIII, which is, of course, an incorrect notation, but was (is) often made this way for better symmetry on the dial.

Men's wristwatches, especially from the 1940s, even up to the 1950s, were tiny compared to today's models. This makes it difficult for the 'real man' to wear them today. They would rather adorn a lady's wrist, but I am afraid that most of the female population would also consider them to be too small. Producers, at the time, wanted to impress with their skills of making watches smaller, also with square cases, and thus away from the appearance and dimensions of a pocket watch.

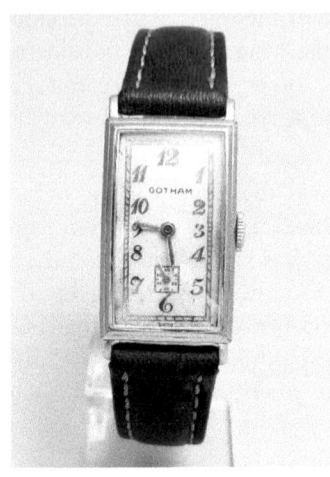

Left and below: 1930s/1940s GOTHAM, by Ollendorf Watch Co., USA, size (h/v): 20mm x 32mm.

The case of this 1940s watch is easy to snap open. That's extremely convenient when doing a cleaning job, but not so ideal what concerns waterproofness.

The acrylic crystal on these watches, used into the present day (more on affordable watches lately), makes it easy to deal with smaller and not so deep scratches.

Speaking of scratches, a lot of people still think they can be polished out. Polishing is for removing dirt and deposits on the surface, a scratch goes into it. In this case, the surrounding material must be brought (sanded) down to this level. Sanding (ultra-fine grid, staring with 1500, then 2000), and polishing with a special paste doing the rest of the job, restores many scratched acrylic dials. There are also special products available to do the job on real glass (filling and polishing), but this involves a more delicate and risky procedure with an uncertain outcome.

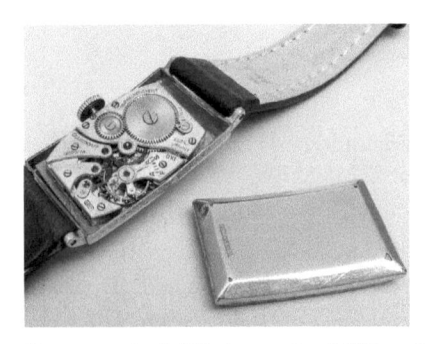

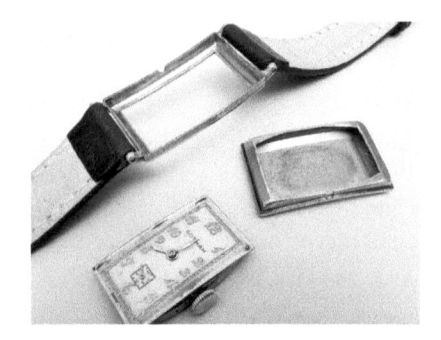

Case marked Wadsworth, 10K gold filled, size without crown and lugs, size (h/v): 20mm x 31mm. Modified (bridges) FEF cal. 130/140 family.

Movement marks: Swiss, Ollendorf Watch Co., 17 jewels, US import code 'IXO' (for Ollendorf Watch Co., USA).

Above left and right: 2nd half of the 1940s GOTHAM (Ollendorf Watch Co., USA), size without crown and lugs (h/v): 27mm x 28mm.

Case marked: 10K R.G.P (rolled gold plated), stainless steel back.

Movement Reconvilier cal. 120 (Swiss). Markings: US import code 'GXI' for Gotham (Ollendorf Watch Co.), New York, RUNJ 63826, Swiss, seven jewels.

Above left and right: 1934 WALTHAM (Waltham, USA), model L-7.25, 1934, size without crown and lugs (h/v): 21mm x 32mm.

Case marked: 10 K gold filled, inside: Keystone, J. Boss, 10K gold filled

Movement marked: Waltham USA, 17 jewels, serial number 28646398 = 1934, total production 144.200 pieces. A very nice thing when you collect vintage Waltham watches (and a few other brands offering the same): just with the serial number alone, you get all the information you need as a collector.

Above left and right: 1946 ELGIN DeLuxe, Elgin, USA, movement Elgin cal. 558, case markings (inside): cased and timed by Elgin Nat. Watch Co., 10KT gold filled, 122389. Movement markings: Elgin 558 USA, L 414058, 17 jewels. Dating made easy thanks to the excellent Elgin serial number system, size without crown and lugs (h/v): 22mm x 26mm.

Above left and right: 1950s HALLMARK, Hallmark Watch Co., USA, movement FHF cal. 170, size (h/v): 29mm x 29mm. Shock protected, case by I.D. Watch Case Co., New York, 10K R.G.P. (rolled gold plated), stainless steel back, Swiss, 17 jewels. Waltham declared bankruptcy in 1949, but continued to sell existing stock. In 1958 they got out of the consumer watch business for good. All remaining inventory went to the Hallmark Watch Co. In line with restructuring procedures, offices in New York had been opened to import Swiss watch movements and cases. As the main creditor did not allow the use of the Waltham name, watches could not be sold directly, but through the independent Hallmark company instead. The Waltham brand is still held alive and kicking by Waltham Int. SA., Switzerland, originally founded in 1954 by Waltham, USA.

As already mentioned before, when collecting vintage or antique watches and clocks, it is important to know as much as possible about the watch, like the year of production, the brand, the maker of the movement and case, etc. It is better to have a few watches, fully documented and technically understood, ideally also including specific elements and technical features of the movement, than a pile of timepieces where most of the relevant information is missing.

The 'hunt' for information can be as exciting as the purchase itself, and some discoveries coming up from research can really be electrifying. For example: There is an automatic watch, coming up later in the book (bottom of page 70), of a rather unknown German brand called Blumus. It came as a bargain with scarce information: '*running, keeping time, presumed to be from the 1950s with a Swiss movement inside.*' Could it be more trivial? But then, it was discovered that the movement, made by ETA, was the *first* automatic version they ever made, the mother of their automatic movements so to speak. You are also educating yourself gathering all that information.

It is also nice to follow the history, company chronicles and stories around the product, often revealing interesting facts. In this respect, Wittnauer is a good example, amongst many others of course.

Left: 1950s WITTNAUER, USA, movement Revue (Swiss) cal. 84/1, 17 jewels, marked 'AXA', US import code for Wittnauer Co., USA, size without crown and lugs (h/v): 23mm x 28mm. Case marked 10K G.F. (gold filled), stainless steel back.

Wittnauer was founded in the year 1872. The name Wittnauer Watch Co. was used as from 1885.

The brand soon established itself amongst navigators, researchers, adventurers and astronomers.

'Daredevil' aviator Jimmie Mattern wore a Wittnauer AllProof, when he attempted to fly around the world. Neil Armstrong, the first man on the moon, had one with him on a preceding Gemini mission.

The famous female pilot Amelia Earhart might still have her Wittnauer on the wrist, deep down in the Pacific Ocean, where she got lost in 1937 during her attempt to circle the Earth along the Equator, unless she secretly ran away with her navigator, as some rumors have it.

Vintage ladies' wristwatches are not everybody's cup of tea; I would rather say nobody's. It's a real shame, because if you get a kick out of these little wonder machines called watches, the tiny ladies' watches from the 1950, for instance, should also make you exited, although technically held much simpler, owed to the fact that the space available is rather limited.

The interest of the female end-users is usually not gear towards all the bells and whistles anyway which make a *'real man's'* watch.

In one respect however, they can serve a good purpose: When discussions come up again if one of those small vintage wristwatches from the 1940s or 1950s is really a men's watch, a ladies' watch can be brought up for comparison to demonstrate how much smaller they were in these days. The left image on the bottom shows a comparison between a ladies' watch from the 1950s and a gents' watch from the 1940s (as shown and described on page 42).

Left: 1940s/1950s SECO, Germany, ladies' wristwatch, case by Kasper (Germany), movement by Felsa (Swiss) cal. 302, 15 jewels, gold plated case. Size without crown and mounting brackets (h/v): 16mm x 23 mm.

Above, left: The small 1940s Gotham, USA, men's watch on the right (20mm x 32mm) looks relatively big compared the SECO ladies' watch to its left (20mm x 23 mm). **Above, right**: The same tiny ladies' watch compared to a ladies' Roamer watch, Switzerland, from the 1960s. And even today, they also have small ladies' watches within their product line; obviously someone must still like them that way.

Left: 1948 BULOVA (code 48), USA, gold plated, movement Bulova cal. 8AH, Dewey case from 1948, size (h/v): 23mm x 27mm.

As the hour markers and the brand name appear in relief, it was possible to polish everything off from a dial which was, unlike the watch itself, not in best condition anymore.

Not exactly what you would call a re-dial (good or badly restored), but not in original condition anymore, nevertheless looking nice and elegant.

More and more watches came along again in the 1950s with round cases. Initially, square cases had been favored, also to have a differentiation from the optical appearance of a pocket watch.

Above left: 1950s JUNGHANS, Germany, movement Junghans cal. J98, case chrome plated and stainless-steel back, Ø 31mm.

Above right: 1957 BULOVA (code L7) Aerojet, USA, gold plated, movement Bulova cal. 11ACC, Ø 35mm. Marking on the case back is M5=1965, the movement is marked L7=1957. Something must have been swapped, which is rather disturbing for an ambitious collector. In superb condition otherwise. Beautiful dress watch, when knowing just the time is enough, perhaps during a nice dinner.

Left: 1950s ROAMER, Swiss, movement MST (Roamer) cal. 372, Roamer Watch SA., Solothurn, Switzerland, gold plated, central seconds indication, Ø 33mm.

The dating of the watch can be done by looking at the logo on the dial. The watch shows the old Roamer version used from 1950 to 1957/58 until Rolex complained that the RW with the five spikes on top looks too similar to their own logo, the five-pointed crown. The year of manufacture can therefore be put between these dates. The movement cal. 372 was produced between 1944 and 1962.

Above left: 1950s ONSA, Swiss, movement HB (Hermann Becker, Germany) cal. 120, gold plated, central seconds indication, size (h/v): 23mm x 27mm.

The watches were getting bigger, but the square form was still popular and an element of distinction from the optical appearance of pocket watches.

Above right: 1950s ONSA, Swiss, movement Arogno (Swiss) cal. 151, gold plated, decentral seconds indication, Ø 33mm. Also here, you can see the often used 'watchmaker's 4' = Roman numeral IV written as IIII, for a better symmetry on the dial.

48

Onsa was founded in 1923 in Lengnau, Switzerland. Good marketing, like sponsoring car races shortly after the war, made the brand popular.

The best promotional 'stunt' was made, when the Mayflower II, a reproduction of the original Mayflower which has brought the first pilgrim to America, crossed the Atlantic, leaving Plymouth, England, on April 20, 1957, and arriving in New York on July 1, 1957. On this trip, two Onsa watches were tested for their water tightness. One of them hung up on the top of the mast in wind and weather, another one was attached under water to the rudder.

Hannes Keller had an Onsa on his wrist when he was diving into the famous Lago Maggiore (the great lake) in the North of Italy, setting a new world record at the time with 155 meters. End of the 1950s, the pilots of Sabena, the Belgian airline, had been equipped with Onsa watches. A large variety of movements, from different manufacturers, can be found in their watches.

The quartz crisis also troubled this company, but they struggled through and came back to success with a lot of standard- and unique models of watches. Since its foundation, the product line includes chronographs, watches with bio-rhythm indication, wristwatches, also with alarm function, and pocket watches.

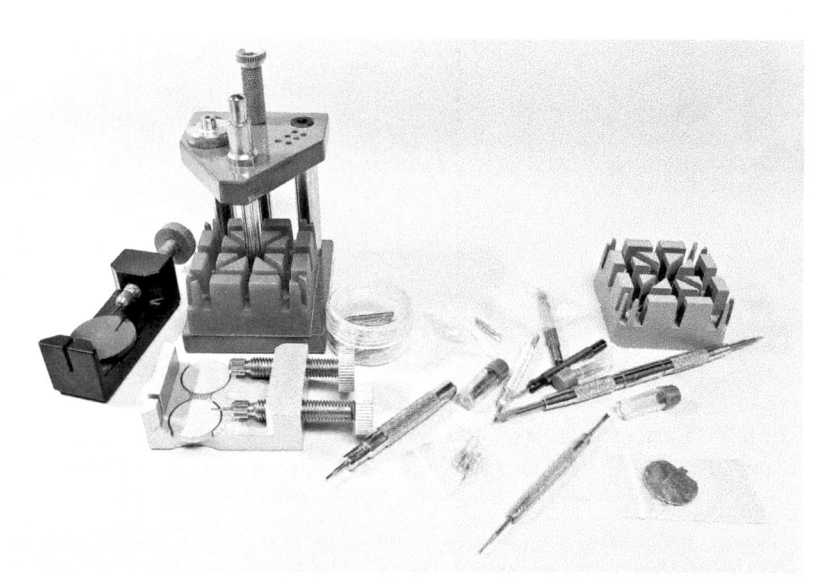

Above: tools for removing links from metal wristbands or changing spring bars.

Above left and right: early 1960s, LA CLOCHE, Swiss, stainless steel case, movement AS (Swiss) cal. 1686, Ø 33mm.

LaCloche (French: the bell) is a brand name of Emilie Quartier Fils, small watches, Aux Brenets, Switzerland, registered 1900. Case marked W. Bell Co., Walter Bell & Co., watches and jewelry, Rockville, Maryland, USA. Originally sold in the USA.

Above left: Left: 1960s TISSOT Visodate Camping, Swiss, gold plated, movement Tissot 782/1 (date), Ø 35mm. The designation 'Camping' most likely suggests some kind of water-tightness, sufficient for outdoor activities.

Above right: 1960s BELECO, Swiss, gold plated, movement Standard (Swiss) cal. 1686, identical with AS 1686, Ø 33mm.

Above left: 1968 BULOVA (code M8), USA, gold plated, movement Bulova cal. 11ALC, Ø 35mm.

Above right: 1960s INGRAHAM, USA, case chrome plated, stainless steel case, movement Kienzle (Germany) caliber 058b25, Ø 34mm. Ingraham – E. Ingraham Co., Bristol, Conn., USA, was founded in 1860 and combined several manufacturers of clocks, where Ingraham was involved before. Pocket watches had been added to the line of production, equipped with third party movements, before Ingraham made its own after 1865. When the time came, they also produced wristwatches. Ingraham is more well known for larger clocks and alarm-clocks. Later, the production had shifted to fuses, which Ingraham started to make during WWII. The imported movement inside this watch comes from Kienzle, Germany. It is one of their few models of pallet lever escapements made, as Kienzle was primarily producing pin lever escapements for the mass market.

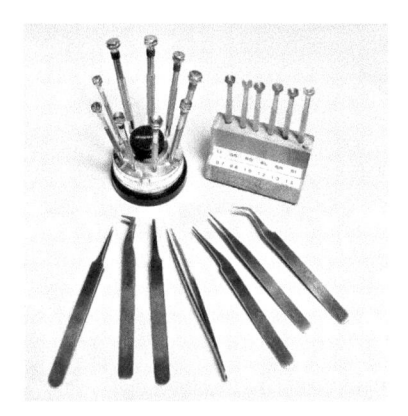

Above: screwdrivers and tweezers, watchmaker's cabinet.

Above left: late 1960s EVERITE, England, gold plated, movement Peseux (Swiss) caliber 7040, f = 21,600 A/h, Ø 33mm. Everite is a brand of the jeweler-chain H. Samuel, Manchester, UK. The watches have been produced for them elsewhere.

Above right: late 1960s EVERITE, England, gold plated, movement Peseux (Swiss) caliber 7066, Ø 33mm. This watch is identical with the one on the left, except that it also shows the date.

Above left: 1960s ARSA, Swiss, gold plated, movement Arsa caliber 1802 / AS ST 1802/03, Ø 34mm. Arsa = Manufacture d'Horologerie A. Reymond SA (Arsa = Auguste Reymond), watches and parts, Tramelan-Dessus, Switzerland.

Above right: 1960s ROAMER Searock, Swiss, gold plated, movement MST (Roamer) cal. 802, Ø 35mm.

Above left and right: 1970s FAVRE-LEUBA Twin Barrel, Swiss, gold plated, movement Favre-Leuba cal. 251, Ø 35mm.

Favre-Leuba is an interesting brand with a very long history. The cornerstone of the company was laid by Abraham Favre in the year 1737, in Le Locle, Switzerland. Through marriage and co-operation with Leuba, the name became Favre-Leuba in the 19th century. The company appeared on the market with a lot of innovative products and operated successfully, until they were also hit by the quartz crisis around the year 1969. The family sold the company, which changed hands a few times afterwards. Since 2011, they are part of an Indian group, the headquarters of Favre-Leuba, however, are still in Switzerland.

Collectors often stay far away from this brand, just because of so many dreadful fake Favre-Leuba watches coming from India ('Bombay-Specials'), which are either cobbled together or complete fakes and sold on the world's Internet platforms. With dials in terrible colors and horrible printing, like made from a children's stamping set, they should better go straight away to the pharmaceutical sector where they could be sold as emetics. Favre-Leuba exported watches to India as the first Swiss producer at a very early stage and they became vastly popular. To make things clear: This has nothing to do with the well-made new products of Favre-Leuba operating in Switzerland today (under Indian ownership).

The above watch is technically highly interesting. It has a twin barrel (double mainspring with two housings). Favre-Leuba wanted to make an ultra-flat watch with a central seconds hand. The latter adds to the height (unlike with a flat watch and a decentral seconds hand). When they found out that the mainspring, which also had to be somewhat flatter, does not deliver enough power anymore, they put in a second one, both coupled in parallel.

There are a lot of weird stories around about this movement, praising superior qualities of its construction which it doesn't have. It did not improve any overall performance and was in the end just a workaround to come to this ultra-flat design – admittedly a brilliant one.

Left: 1968 GLYCINE Altus, Swiss, gold plated, movement AS (Swiss) cal. 1686, Ø 34mm.

'La Glycine' (French for the climbing plant wisteria), was founded under this name in 1914. Famous in the early years for extremely small ladies' watches. They made their first automatic watch already in 1931. Later, they came out with watches for heavy duty use. Since the 1990s, they are widely known for their Airman watches. The company survived the quartz crisis and soon got back to its position as specialist for mechanical watches, when the market was ready again for highly priced timepieces.

Above left and right: 1970s to 1980s no name watch, gold plated, movement UMF (East Germany) cal. 24, Ø 34mm. Not really a collector's item, but also a piece of watchmaking history. When the companies in the former DDR lost their independence, it was more or less over with the high art of watchmaking. Nevertheless, a lot of watches and movements went versus the West and into the lower market segment to get urgently needed foreign currency. This watch was a giveaway by a vacuum cleaner sales representative to his clients. Whatever you might want to say, the movements were reliable, uncomplicated and durable. Simple pin lever escapement, no shock protection, no jewels, no compensating balance, movement (one size fits all) held by a plastic ring and a sheet metal holder with bendable noses (did I hear somebody say Timex M24?). VEB (nationally owned company) Uhren und Maschinenfabrik (UMF), Ruhla, Thuringia, East Germany produced 130 million movements of this cal. 24 family between 1963 and 1990. If you are not into wearing a precise quartz watch, but prefer something more rudimentary, that's all the watch you need – that's like eating raw meat!

Top left and right: 1968 ROTARY, Swiss, gold plated, movement AS (Swiss), cal. 1901, Ø 33mm.

Bottom left and right: 1970s ROTARY, Swiss, gold plated, movement France Ebauches (France), cal. 140, Ø 34mm.

The Rotary brand was under different ownership over the years, also with different production sites. Both watches above come from Rotary – Moise Dreyfuss, Fabrique Enila, Fabrique de Montres Rotary, small watches, watch parts, jewelry, Geneva and La Chaux-de-Fonds, Switzerland, founded 1865.

The logo with the winged wheel was registered in 1926.

Left: 1972 BULOVA, USA, stainless steel 'cushion case', movement Bulova cal. 11AOCD, size (h/v): 36mm x 42mm.

When the watches began to show the date, weekday and even month, it was cumbersome in the beginning to correct everything. Certain types of quick-sets have been developed to facilitate this process. One way to set the date a bit faster, without a special quickset, was by moving the time forward and over midnight, and then, instead of winding forward another 24 hours, the hands were moved back to 9 p.m. and again over midnight (or somewhat further). If there were other indications beside the date, they could later be set directly from a different position of the crown, but often, this was messing up previous settings again if all was not done in the right order. On this watch, the date can be set a lot easier by repeatedly pulling and pushing the crown.

All these additional indications (or complications) of a watch, like day, date, months or the moon phase, have always been a major source of defects, when people were fiddling around without an instructions manual at hand, mostly not available when a vintage watch was acquired. There are also specific time periods in which no setting should be done (no-set-periods) – a certain phase before midnight, when the watch is already preparing to shift the disks.

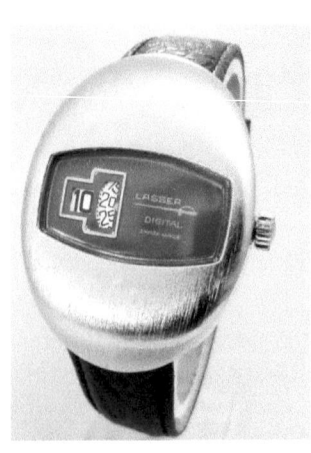

Left: 1970s LASSER 'Jump Hour', Swiss, gold plated, size (h/v): 34mm x 46mm, NOS – from new old stock, movement BF (Baumgartner) cal. 582, pin-lever, 1 jewel.

This watch is an interesting, although ugly example of a so-called jump hour watch. Digital display (leaving aside modern LEDs and LCDs) has been around for long and can even be found on antique watches. The hour disk on this watch *'jumps'* ahead every hour. The minute disk moves continuously.

Here, the designation 'NOS' must raise some questions. NOS (new old stock), means merchandise which has never been in the hands of an end-user, forgotten in storage or never sold before for some reason. When you then see identical watches (also other variations) coming up on the Internet platforms in large quantities, it is hard to believe that they all are really 'genuine' new old stock; perhaps a re-make, perhaps produced from old parts still lying around.

Left: 1980s CATOREX Skeleton watch, Swiss, gold plated, movement based on Peseux (Swiss) cal. 7040, Ø 32mm.

Catorex is well known for their skeleton watches, both pocket- and wristwatches. This one does not only have a glass cover on both sides, the movement is very much 'skeletonized' to provide an optimal view into the movement and showing the work it's doing.

It is quite impressive to see how a movement does its work, keeping the power and accuracy, despite a slackening mainspring. This watch runs at $f = 21,600$ A/h (half beats per hour of the balance wheel) with an amplitude of about 270°, equaling 10,800 full swings with a total of 540 degrees. Translated into 360 degrees, this would be 16,200 full turns per hour, 388,800 per day and about 142 million a year. After 7 years, the wheel will have turned 1 billion (!) times.

Looking at the *'tick and tack'*, the blocking and releasing of the escape wheel with every half beat (21,600 A/h), this adds up to about 189 million actions per year and 1 billion after approx. 5.3 years; respect for the work of a mechanical watch!

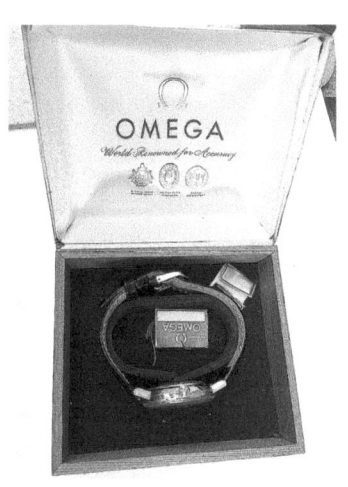

Left: OMEGA watch in the original box.

The value of a vintage watch can substantially increase if the original box is still available, preferably also documents and papers like sales invoice, instructions manual, guarantee certificate (although expired a long time ago) or smaller things like price tags, etc.

It, of course, depends on the type and value of the watch.

In the affordable range, it is rather something nice to have, but for some specific brands, it is more or less essential and can also be proof of authenticity and origin.

WATCH CASES

Wristwatches come in different cases. They can be very simple, like the two-shell cases of the early type, which you just separate to lay open the movement with the dial. Later, in order to have a more effective protection against water and humidity, the cases became better sealed (besides gaskets around the crown), starting with a snap on/off back cover and different screw backs. The best sealed watches are the so-called 'divers' which can not only be used under the shower or in the pool, but also a few hundred meters down into the sea.

Now, you can be faced with serious problems when you try to open a watch case. Of course, this is of little interest to the collector who will always see a watchmaker for that, but the more ambitious watch enthusiast often wants to see what movement caliber is ticking inside (often unknown when watches have been acquired) or to look at different components like the shock protection. Regulating a watch can also only be done when the back is open (or the movement laid bare) and last, but not least, you want to see the movement to judge the condition of a timepiece and see if it is clean or has already gathered rust inside.

Opening such a watch can be a cumbersome task, ranging from difficult to mission impossible, even with the right tools. For some special cases, the usual case openers can't do the job, not to speak of a cover seized-up by dirt, etc.

But it is not always just a thing to do in the back. Some cases, especially designed for better waterproofness, are made in such a way, that the movement comes out only through the front, which means that you first have to take off the crystal, and then you deal with the removal of the stem by tearing it apart (split stem), as you cannot remove/release it in one piece at the back. On some watches, you also have to remove the hands and the dial to proceed further.

In other words, you might be faced with a watch that cannot be opened without special knowledge and tools or the back is more or less stuck forever. You often see watches with scratched backs, which is a clear indication that someone has had problems opening it. A movement shot, not shown at an Internet auction, usually a reason to be very skeptical, could also be due to the fact, that the seller had trouble opening it, often unable to tell what movement is inside. As an unexperienced collector, you should at first avoid such watches, unless you are willing to take the risk about the condition or have no interest in the technical features inside, including the movement caliber, or you have a friendly watchmaker at hand close by. Of course: High priced and luxury watches are something different, as you should not fiddle around with them in any case.

Normally, if not sitting too tight, you should be able to open most screw back watches with a suction ball, cheaply available on the Net, or a device with a suction cap, which could however require a first step with a regular opening tool to get it loose.

SHOCK PROTECTION

If a watch is marked, 'anti-shock', shock-protected', 'super-shock', etc. on the dial, it means it has a shock protection. You might also find nothing at all or perhaps a marking on the back. Often, the type of shock protection is indicated with the maker or brand name of this device, like 'Incabloc', one of the big names in the industry in Switzerland, besides KIF-Parechoc. Today this is standard and more seldom – if at all – mentioned on the dial.

If a watch is dropped or knocked, the shock can cause the balance staff pivots to bend or break. Especially pocket watches and earlier wristwatches are affected by this problem. It was a common thing in the earlier days and one of the major areas of repair for watchmakers.

To deal with the problem, different systems have been developed. First practical applications came shortly before and after the end of the 18th century. The best known and most widely used system is 'Incabloc', invented by Fritz Marti, a Swiss engineer, in the 1920s. All systems work basically in the same fashion. The jewels of the balance staff are supported by small springs instead of being fixed firmly to the plates. **Image above: Incabloc.** Keeping the initial principle, with continuous improvements in the production process, ensures the highest quality standards over the long term.

Despite all the advantages, adoption was very slow overall. Again, it was the military setting the pace. A broken watch of a taxman is less of a problem than in a maneuver or serious action. And what the military has, every man wants to have too, like a diver watch under the shower or the pilots watch for the occasional passenger in the economy class.

Above left: no shock-protection. **Above right:** shock protection (Incabloc).

COMPENSATING BALANCE, SCREW BALANCE

Left: example of a bi-metallic compensation balance / screw balance.

The need for precise watches used for the navigation at sea was a driving force to improve the construction of the balance wheel.

Already in the year 1753, a compensating balance was used in the famous H4 of the Englishman John Harrison. It was gradually improved by later watchmakers, like the French horologist Pierre LeRoy or the Englishman Thomas Earnshaw.

Temperature is an element influencing the beat of a watch, causing an expansion or a contraction of the balance wheel. Most of this problem has been solved with the upcoming of the bi-metallic compensating balance. The outer rim of the balance, which is divided into two parts, is a sandwich layer of steel and brass, which react differently to temperature changes (the thermal expansion of brass is greater than that of steel).

A compensating balance is mostly combined with a screw balance. The screws around can be adjusted to cope with possible imbalances. The latter construction has actually become superfluous today, due to better materials used and parts made with higher precision. They are nevertheless still made this way in today's high-grade mechanical watches, as this is seen as a sign of quality in watchmaking.

Above: case back press for those hard to close snap on lids

MAGNETISM AND WATCHES

Pay attention to your surroundings when wearing or storing a watch in the vicinity of magnetic fields. Although magnetism in (mechanical) watches plays and ever smaller role as we move forward in time, it is still something we must be concerned about, even today. For the collector of vintage wristwatches, not to speak of antique- and vintage pocket watches, it's a really seriously issue.

'Antimagnetic' is a term one often finds on vintage watches or even models of newer date, but that doesn't mean that the watch is fully antimagnetic – far away from it and only up to a certain extent, on whatever basis manufacturers come up which such a designation.

Newer watches are generally less vulnerable to magnetism. In recent years, better materials are used and some mechanical watches meet the minimum anti-magnetic standards, up to high-grade watches which far exceed those benchmarks. But here, we are talking about names like Rolex, IWC, Sinn, Bremont, Damasko or Omega. The latter claim to have the first absolutely non-magnetic watch, which can withstand magnetic fields up to 15.000 Gauss. An even higher certification could have been reached, but that needed testing equipment which was not available. Above 10,000 Gauss, another unit is used, called Tesla (10,000 Gauss = 1 Tesla).

Despite being powered by almost ancient spring technology, the mechanical watch is still one of the most complex machines ever made by man. But some, definitively highly respectable developments in watchmaking, leave the impression, as if someone has invented a new concentrated fodder for horses with the aim to improve transport by stage coach. All that, in competition to cheap and very accurate quartz watches or the radio-controlled watches, working at a precision of +/- 1 second possible deviation in millions of years, based on a signal coming from a single atomic clock and regulating individual watches at somebody's wrist.

Quartz watches are only temporarily affected by magnetism and whilst in the magnetic field. Digital types are quite safe, analogue types could become problems with the gear-mechanism of the hands. When the quartz watch is out of the magnetic field, it should resume its normal functioning. In a mechanical watch however, magnetism remains inside the watch if moved away. It mainly (but not only) affects the hairspring which, together with the balance and escapement, is regulating the clocking of the watch.

Hard to believe, but true: There is an area making certain mechanical watches still superior to quartz watches. In a working environment like at CERN, the European nuclear research center in Geneva, Switzerland, a quartz watch will stop working, but a mechanical watch, effectively shielded against magnetism, will continue to run with precision, like the Rolex Milgauss, developed by request of CERN in the 1950s (Milgauss = withstanding mille gauss or 1,000 gauss, the number considered necessary by CERN).

There are numerous sources of magnetism around us, be it large loudspeakers or smaller ones (distance needs to be closer here), diagnostic- and medical equipment, monitors, IT- and computer equipment, mobile phones, frequent flying in higher altitudes, cell phones, laptops, hard disks, security systems, microwave ovens – you name it.

An old Waltham pocket watch, with a recent full service, had never shown any problems, until it was running fast for an unknown reason, even after regulating it down as far as possible. It went to the watchmaker and came back, without him charging anything; it was just a quickly solved matter of de-magnetization. A few days later, after testing it at home, the same problem occurred again. The solution: it was before put on a stand next to a PC-loudspeaker and left in the same place again, after it came back.

Magnetizing affects the hairspring regulating the vibrations/clocking of the watch. It sticks together, caused by magnetizing, which makes it 'pump' faster. There is an equal effect when the spring got dirty or oily. If nothing else is wrong, the watch stays accurate – just accurately imprecise. Strong magnetic fields are not damaging the watch, but can strongly influence its accuracy or even stop it. They alter not only the functioning of the balance spring; other metallic components inside are even more sensitive and create magnetic fields themselves inside the watch. Low-intensity fields will result in a slight disturbance of the watch's regular functioning, often not immediately noticed, but soon leading to the assumption, that there is something wrong with the watch mechanically.

What about isochronism you might say, which always keeps a watch in beat? Well, it's the other way around here. We have learned that according to the laws of isochronism, pendulums of the same length (the balance of a watch works alike) are always swinging at equal time intervals, independent from their distance of travel. The effect of magnetism is however like shortening a pendulum, which obviously makes it swing faster.

What concerns the magnetization of hairsprings, the effect was mitigated with an invention made around the mid 1930s. Reinhard Staumann, a Swiss engineer, had developed a new metal alloy, mainly for the watch industry, called NIVAROX – German: **ni**cht **var**iabel **ox**ydfest (not variable resistant to oxidation), made of nickel, chromium, manganese, titanium, beryllium, silicon and iron.

The hairsprings made out of Nivarox are also less sensitive to temperature changes. Reinhard Stauman took no rest to solve also the problems of another spring inside the watch, the driving force – the mainspring. They had been susceptible to corrosion and at risk of breakage. In the year 1948, he had found the right mixture: cobalt, nickel, chromium, iron, tungsten and molybdenum, with traces of titanium and beryllium (sounds like a French cooking experiment with different ingredients). The name of the new material for the mainsprings: NIVAFLEX.

What do we do when a watch is suddenly running fast or comes from an Internet platform as *'gains a few minutes a day, might need service'*?

Besides taking the balance wheel with the hairspring out to give it a cleaning (delicate task), one could at first check if magnetizing is the cause of the problem and fix it with the right instrument.

But before taking any of these steps, how can you determine that a watch is really magnetized? There is a very simple method by using a compass: move around with the watch and see if it distracts the needle. This can also be done as a routine matter with the delicate screwdrivers or tweezers before working on a watch.

For demonstration purposes (see next page), two compasses have been placed next to each other. They should, without any external influences, both point in the same direction. A magnetized screwdriver was placed next to one of them to show the effect (it wouldn't make sense to magnetize a watch for this demonstration). Of course, for testing purposes at home, one compass is enough.

You see, more intensively dealing with watches, even just as a collector, often makes you also a 'watchmaker' to some extent, often with a growing workshop. Step by step, you can save time (and respect the watchmaker as a highly qualified expert for demanding tasks) by doing a few things yourself and be it just the changing of a wristband with an encore of new spring bars.

Demagnetizing the hairspring can be done in different ways, with self-made instruments, use of de-magnetizers originally intended for other use like the old hand-held tool for de-magnetizing audio heads or professional instruments which are usually very expensive. But you can have the best of both worlds if you get an affordable, yet reliable quality instrument. In any case, avoid some of the cheap trash floating around. Here, this crap is not simply useless, but can severely damage the watch.

Left: Late 1950s SMITHS Astral mil issue – protected against magnetism.

Made in England, stainless steel case, movement Smiths cal. 12.15, Ø 35mm.

Not only flying the flag of British watchmaking, but also something special concerning early measures taken against the effect of magnetization on a watch. It has a mu-metal dial and -dust cover inside, which form a protective anti-magnetic Faraday cage around the movement.

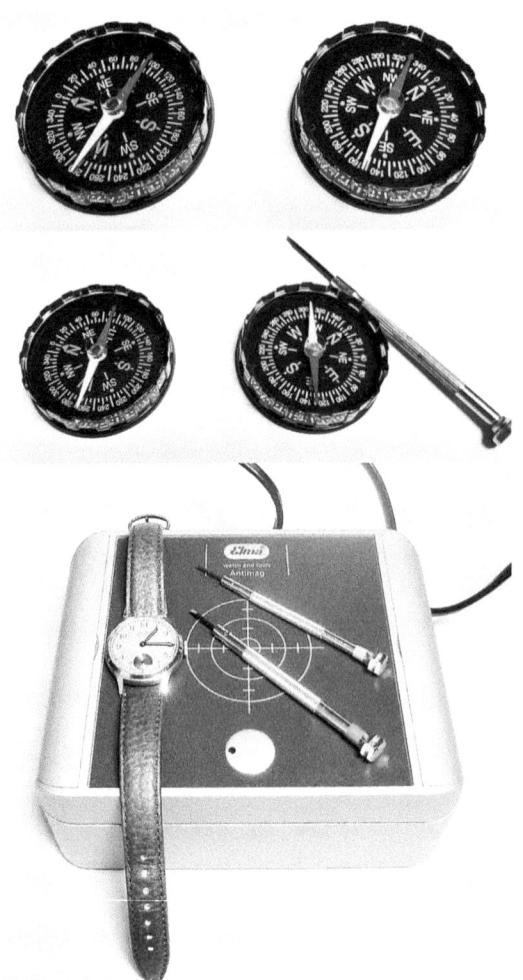

Left, top: Both compasses point in the same direction.

Left, middle: A magnetized screwdriver was put next to one of them and the needle turned by almost 180° towards the magnetic source. In a video, it could be shown how the needle follows the screwdriver around.

Left, bottom: A highly effective de-magnetizing tool in the affordable range.

It takes just one touch of a bottom to de-magnetize the object lying on the top.

Smaller parts have to be put into a bag, as they will jump up when the button is pressed.

The device shuts itself off within a fraction of a second, whilst the finger is still on the button, no time to be observed, no slow removal of the object to whatever distance and other things you have to do with cheap or impractical stuff.

When intentionally magnetizing a watch for testing purposes, which is then demagnetized again, one can compare the different performances, before and after, on the timegrapher. It goes from a total mess on the display, with dots all over the place like on a starry sky, not showing any +/- deviations anymore, with an inability to pick up the amplitude automatically, and then back to acceptable, straight dotted lines and sensible results after de-magnetization, provided that everything else is in an acceptable state.

ADJUSTMENT AND REGULATION OF A WATCH

The regulation of a watch should be something of interest to every serious collector. After all, the recently purchased watch from an Internet platform might not be so bad after all – or even worse. We are talking here about mechanical watches with lever escapement. Other escapements, like the cylinder escapement, are a different issue, for instance the behavior on the timegrapher.

Adjustment and regulation – although the terms are often used for the same thing, there is a difference between the two. An adjustment is the more complicated procedure, where you also have to observe the order in which things are done. Regulating is simply moving the regulator to make the watch run faster or slower by changing the length of the active part of the hairspring. Adjusting also involves other things like the positioning of the balance's hairspring (synchronization of tick and tack), the balancing of the balance wheel or perhaps also shaping the balance pivots. Some regulating mechanisms let you influence both, the length of the active part of the hair spring and its position.

Left: regulation with two levers, allowing the adjustment of the beat (positioning of the hairspring) and the regulation of the frequency (length of the active part of the spring).

The watch can either be out of beat (no synchronism between tick and tack) and/or run fast or slow. There could be something wrong with the movement in many places, or all is only a matter of adjustment and/or regulation. Needless to say, that doing these things without having the movement cleaned first, the jewels or bearings lubricated, etc. (watchmaker service job), will not be an ideal and longer lasting solution. A timegrapher is an absolute must, even for the sole regulation of the active length and/or position of the hairspring, to get fast results and corresponding feedback.

Whatever, moving the regulator pin or lever back and forth, to make a watch run faster or slower, can be done with a minimum level of skill. Some contemporaries might also visit their watchmaker shortly after closing of his shop and show him the watch through the window, whilst he is signaling from the inside that the store is closed and then go to the Internet and sell the precious piece as *'time adjusted, seen by a watchmaker'*.

Left: regulation with just one movable lever, allowing to regulate the frequency (length of the active part of the spring). Adjustments to the beat (position of the hairspring) cannot be done directly.

Simpler constructed regulations mostly do not provide for the possibility of a quick adjustment of the hairspring's position, but just its active length. Here, everything must be taken out to make corrections. As the hairspring with the balance wheel can't always go in and out until a satisfactory result is achieved, a special device is needed to test and fix that externally. It's an expensive tool and some experience is necessary to do this. Here, for all practical purposes, one has to restrict himself to the regulation of the length of the balance spring, to make it pump faster or slower. At the sides of the regulator, there are markings 'F and 'S' (for Fast and Slow) or the French version 'A' and 'R' (Avance and Retard (advance and delay) and occasionally just a '+' and '-'.

Left: regulation of a pocket watch with a long pin (lever) allowing to regulate the frequency (length of the active part of the spring). Adjustments to the beat (position of the hairspring) can also not be done directly.

Look at the regulator pin's position when you see the movement of a watch you might want to purchase. If it's all the way to the maximum versus 'fast', it's not a good sign and the movement would need a cleaning and lubrication at the minimum.

The other way around (watch running fast), it could be somewhat less dramatic and perhaps just a matter of magnetization or a dirty and sticky hairspring. Watch collectors speak of a good sign if the needle is pointing *'straight to the South'* (right in the middle). Another thing is to look at the hairspring itself if the watch is running fast and the usual causes can be excluded. At the outer end, it is usually held by a screw or by a little conical pin (in the case of older pocket watches). If you don't see anything of the spring sticking out, it might have been broken at the end and scantily re-inserted with whatever was left. Then, it is simply too short altogether. In the sense of just briefly touching this subject, a lot of more specific things like deformations of the hairspring, etc. must be left out.

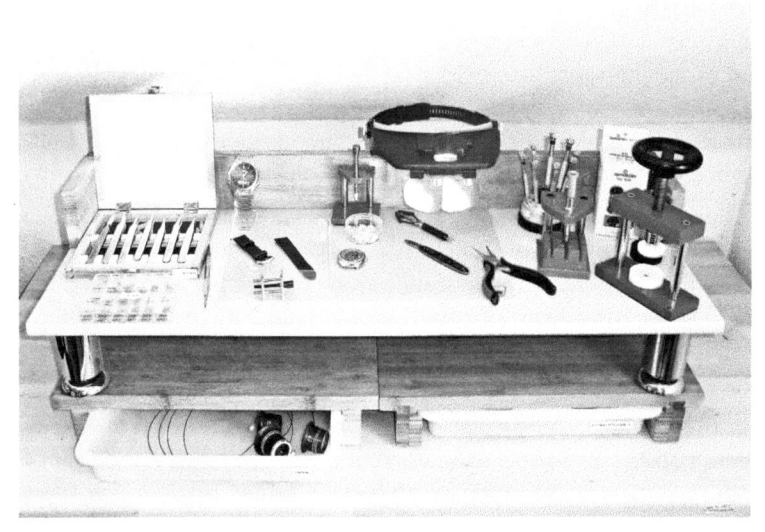

Small portable watchmaker's workbench: With some practice, one can start with small jobs like changing wristbands or batteries, cleaning tasks or polishing of acrylic crystals, etc. More complicated tasks can eventually be tackled with enough experience and training.

The Sushi cutting boards found a new use here by further lifting the working surface.

When you see all those images with watchmakers having the working height going up to their chin, don't worry. When you do a few jobs at 'lower levels', right on your normal desk, that's all right. Working in these 'high altitudes', in an upright seating posture, with the watch right in front of the nose, is more ergonomic and better for the back in the long run, especially during long working hours in the assembly process or in the watchmaker's shop. You can write an e-mail whilst lying on the couch, but you should give your secretary the right chair and desk when she is typing your letters all day long.

CONDITION OF WATCH DIALS

The dial is the face of the watch; for many collectors, it is considered to be a very important, if not the most important part, provided that it is otherwise in technically good order.

Gunk or patina, fine aging or ruined, the opinions differ like the taste. Whatever, a dial in bad shape is really a watch in bad shape. Flaking lacquer, water stains, scratches, blotches and whatever, can make a watch look extremely ugly. In some cases, wear and tear or an aged dial must not be so dramatic in view of a history and the former use of the watch, or when someone might acquire it solely for its technical features, but otherwise, it can (and mostly will) substantially reduce the value of a watch, down to its last use for spare parts.

Look at a watch before buying and ask yourself, would it look nice in your collection or would it just be stored away in a box of cheaply acquired curiosities? Would you wear it; can you wear it without leaving the impression that you spend the nights sleeping under a bridge? Would someone else buy it from you again and at what price?

The condition of a dial can range from pristine to beat-up. It could be fully and partly restored, but often you don't know what it should look like in its original condition without enough experience. Re-done or re-finished means that someone has worked on it, often with dreadful results. Beginners usually do not notice all the deficiencies, too often not even if the renovated dial comes from a restorer's horror cabinet with spelling errors.

There are professional and specialized restorers who can do an excellent job. But here, where good results can be assumed, it is predominantly a matter of price in relation to the value of the watch (unless it's a family heirloom or connected to special memories).

Some amateurs have admittedly developed good skills in that respect; many different methods all have their pros and cons, often with a highly unpredictable outcome, and in the end, many of such 'restorations' go wrong, often badly wrong.

However, if you are happy with the 'patina' (the term was created in the middle of the 18th century from the Italian word for 'coating'), no matter where it comes from, what it is and why it's there – go ahead! After all, some of those tasteless and kitschy-gilded Louis XVI fireplace clocks have stood in bordellos for decades – wow, that's exiting!

But what can you do? Don't buy such a watch in the first place if you want to start a serious collection without any hassle, at least in the beginning.

Of course, you can make it a hobby (or profession) to restore watches and dials, but that should not be the starting point. A handful of well-kept timepieces, also optically in best shape, is a lot more fun than piling up on scruffy watches.

MECHANICAL WRISTWATCHES, AUTOMATIC

To do away with the frequent need for periodical winding, engineers have put their efforts into the development of something that would replace the manual procedure, which was finally made superfluous with the upcoming of the battery driven watches; but before, other ways have been found to do the winding automatically, and all came back with the revival of the mechanical watches.

Watches can automatically be wound up in several ways, like making use of changing temperature. The Atmos, a desk clock model made by Jaeger-LeCoultre since the 1930s, needs a difference in temperature of just 1° within the range of 15° to 30° Celsius to give the watch the power to run for an additional 48 hours. This watch became the official Swiss state gift.

Another method is to use the movements of the human body, and especially those of the wrist, to give power to the wristwatches. The mainspring is frequently wound up by the motions of the wearer's wrist.

Several techniques have been developed to make use of an eccentric weight that turns on a pivot. This was at first the bumper type (not fully rotating and stopped at the ends by pumpers) and then a semi-circular weight that can fully turn around in either direction (rotor).

A variation of this technique was the mini-rotor, with the circular weight, smaller than the normal one, with a pendulum suspension outside the center. Winding was at first only in one particular direction, left or right, and finally bi-directional. When the watch is out of power after it has been put aside for some time, there is the possibility of conventional winding (here called pre-winding) to give the mainspring some tension to start with.

An automatic watch cannot be overwound. The winding mechanism continues to work even if the watch is fully wound up, without putting excessive tension on the mainspring, which could otherwise even break it. A slipping clutch takes care of this problem. The 'slipping mainspring', as a safety mechanism, was already patented by Adrian Philippe, co-founder of Patek-Philippe, long before any self-winding wristwatches came along. He also invented the crown for winding, replacing the keys.

Automatic windings were first implemented in pocket watches. Reports of first self-winding watches came up already at the end of 1773, but these were most likely some of the stories around the never-ending myth of the perpetuum mobile. Others followed with such a claim, but there isn't any proof that they had a fully working type, until the Swiss watchmaker Abraham-Louis Perrelt from Le Locle came along around the year 1777 with the invention of a self-winding mechanism. 15 minutes walking were necessary to wind up the pocket watch.

Many other names could be mentioned here and the different models, coming over time, really worked and had been produced, but everything has remained more or less exotic for more than 100 years, before the wristwatches came along.

And finally, the movement of the wrist was supplemented by watch winders, which take care of the power reserve if the watch is not frequently worn.

Watch winder: Automatic watches are wound up by the movement of the wrist. If they are worn every day, it doesn't matter if they are put away at night. The power reserve is more than sufficient for such short interruptions. If the power has run down, automatic watches can be pre-wound and are ready to run again immediately, but everything, mostly not only the time, has to be set again.

Especially when watches have a lot of indications, like day, weekday, month or moon-phase, this can be quite a challenging and time-consuming task.

All of it can be avoided by putting the watch on a watch winder when not in use. It runs at intervals, left, right or bi-directional, with a certain number of turns per day.

There are frequent arguments amongst watch collectors if one should have such a device (or more of them) or not – keeping the watch going and partly preventing the drying out of oils – versus better leaving it alone.

The winder shown can also be operated on batteries, which makes it ideal for the treasured and seldom worn 'safe queen', without a cable hindering the closing of the door.

Above left and right: 1954 (L4) BULOVA Automatic, USA, gold plated case, movement Bulova cal. 10BOAC, 23 jewels, Ø without lugs 31mm.

Year after year Bulova came out with so many different, mostly fancy cases, making it virtually impossible to keep track. No other manufacturer came close to such abundance, if not to say oodles of new case models, especially in the 1930s, 1940s and 1950s. This is a very popular version of Bulova self-winding watches with nice, fancy lugs.

Above left and right: 1950s BLUMUS DeLuxe Automatic, Germany, gold plated, movement ETA (Swiss), cal. 1256, Ø without lugs 33mm.

Blumus = Adolf Bluemelink, Munich, Germany, registered 1927, watch by Silvana, Fabrique d'Horologerie Silvana SA, V.E. Bahon, Tramelan Dessus, Switzerland.

The movement inside is the first automatic movement ever made by ETA (1950/51), already with bi-directional winding.

Left: 1950s BELLANA Automatic, Germany, gold plated, movement ETA (Swiss) cal. 2461, official watch of the German Railroad Company, Ø 35mm.

According to paragraph 408 of the regulations of the German Railroad Company, every official, to whom this rule applied, had to carry a precisely running watch. This was the same in many other countries.

There are frequent arguments about the term 'precise', as a watch can show the wrong time and still run precise (fast or slow at a constant rate).

Bellana and also Saxonia had produced and sold these watches at reasonable prices up until the 1990s and slightly beyond. The employees had to pay for the watch themselves, but could do that also in installments, directly deducted from the monthly salary. Representatives of the company came into the offices or employee canteens to show the watches, also offering a regular and free inspection or a temporary replacement when necessary. With the upcoming of the cheap and precise quartz-watches, this system became obsolete.

This automatic watch with 30 jewels was most likely worn by the higher ranks.

Above left: 1950s ONSA Automatic, Swiss, gold plated, movement Felsa (Swiss) cal. 4007, 25 jewels, Ø 34mm. **Above right: late 1960s - early 1970s ONSA Superautomatic**, Swiss, case chrome plated, stainless steel back, movement ETA (Swiss) cal. 2453, 30 jewels, Ø 34mm.

Above left: 1959 OMEGA Automatic Seamaster, Swiss, stainless steel case, movement Omega val. 552, 24 jewels, Ø 35mm. A very solid and reliable movement, one of the best of its time, made by Omega from 1958 until 1969, with an unusual frequency of f = 19,800 A/h.

Above right: 1960s OMEGA Automatic Constellation, Swiss, officially certified Chronometer, movement Omega cal. 564, 24 jewels, f = 19,800 A/h, effective date quickset (by pulling the crown), power reserve 50 hours, Ø 35mm.

If you are interested in vintage watches without wanting to start a larger collection and rather concentrate on one a few very specific specimens, this is one of them (amongst several others of course) to get, although not to have 'for a song', that would be more of a longer evening song recital.

The Omega Constellation line of watches, also in other model variations, shows the Cupola of the Geneva observatory with 8 stars around (see example on page 88, picture middle/left). In astronomy, the term 'constellation' refers to a group of stars, moving through the Universe in a consistent and predictable manner. In the case of Omega, the 8 stars represent their greatest chronometric achievements, including the famous *'clean sweep'* of the year 1931, when they broke the records for precision in all categories.

Omega is well represented in sport's timekeeping across the board. Heuer (now Tag Heuer) were the first to officially stop the time at these events in 1920, 1924 and 1928. Before that, each referee brought along his own individual watch.

Since 1932, except for the games in the year 1972 in Munich, Germany, (timing by Junghans), Omega time measurement is linked to the Olympic events. In that year 1932, one watchmaker and thirty caliber 1130 stopwatches in a suitcase made it across the Atlantic and to Los Angeles. This has developed over the years to a few hundred timekeepers, data recording specialists, thousands of trained volunteers, several tons of equipment, scoreboards and miles of cables, to meet the requirements of modern times.

Above left: 1960s ROAMER LimeLight Automatic, Swiss, gold plated case, movement MST (Roamer) cal. 479 = ETA cal. 2622, f = 21,600 A/h, Ø 34mm.

Above right: 1964 TISSOT Seastar Automatic, Swiss, gold plated case, movement Tissot cal. 783, 21 jewels, Ø 34mm. Tissot serial numbers engraved on the movement (here 6702549) are extremely helpful when dating the watch.

Above left: 1970 (N0) BULOVA Automatic, Swiss, gold plated case, movement Bulova cal. 11ANAC, f = 21,600 A/h, Ø (without lugs) 35mm. Nice 'easy read' dial (red seconds hand), indicating the time as a watch should.

Above right: 1970s LANCO Automatic, Swiss, gold plated case, movement Tissot cal. 2481 = Omega 1481, f = 21,600 A/h, very effective date quickset (simple push of the crown to advance by one day), Ø (without lugs) 34mm. The watch was made when Lanco was part of the Omega/Tissot group (SSIH).

Left: 1970s ETERNA, Eterna Matic, Automatic, Swiss, stainless steel, movement Eterna cal. 12824 (ETA 2824), 25 jewels, date, hack feature, f = 28,800 A/h (high beat).

Eterna used an ETA movement as the basis and gave it its own typical rotor (Eterna Rotor) with five bearing balls. These bearing balls also became the Eterna logo, which can be found on the dial and on the crown.

Eterna had used a KIF shock protection in this movement, whilst the ETA version is equipped with an Incabloc.

Above left: 1970s ARISTO Automatic Alarm, Swiss, stainless steel case, movement AS (Swiss) cal. 5008, 25 jewels, F = 28,800 A/h (high beat), day- and date quickset, size (h/v): without lugs 36mm x 36mm. Alarm can be wound and set, activated and silenced, with the 2nd crown at the 4 o'clock position.

Above right: 1970s DELMA Automatic, Swiss, gold plated case, movement ETA (Swiss) cal. 2789, day- and date quickset, German language day disk, size (h/v): 36mm x 36mm. The watch is NOS (from new old stock).

Above left and right: 2003 DUBOIS Automatic, Swiss, gold plated case, movement ETA (Swiss) cal. 2824-2, f = 28,800 A/h (high beat), Ø (without lugs) 34mm.

The watch has an open balance, visible from the front, and a glass back, allowing a view into the movement. The ETA high quality movement 2824-2 is very reliable and used in watches of many brands. It is a so called high-beat watch with 28.800 half beats per hour.

DuBois (Dubois & Fils), founded 1785 in Le Locle, Switzerland, is the oldest watch manufacturer in the country (not the oldest watchmaker). In recent years, watches were made under license with the DuBois brand name (DuBois 1785) in the higher priced sector, solely produced in Switzerland and mostly sold over the Internet. It is a bit unclear who made them and under whose responsibility, but you seldom see a watch anymore which is 100% Swiss what concerns movement, case, as well as dial and hands. Also, the assembly of the movement, the casing, the regulation of all functions and the factory first inspection was all done in Switzerland. The term 'Made in Switzerland' is not so easy to pin down, especially for watches. The requested genuine Swiss portion is subject to change and also the different areas this should apply to and to what extent. Some even came up with the idea, that the *'Swissness'* of a watch largely depends on the brand and its reputation and to a lesser extend where it is made. Like a Cowboy, who is always a Cowboy, even in Russia. In the year 2013, the brand was re-activated again as a regular watchmaking company through private equity funding and is now concentrating on quality watches with limited editions.

The watch is still unworn and is put on a watch winder every month to keep it running a few days. Despite the problem of oils drying in over time, even if the watch is unused, it shows flawless readings on the timegrapher, absolute precision with a straight line across and nothing out of beat. Even the expensive original wristband has been put aside. Did someone say *'how about wearing it?'*

TIMEX, NEW TECHNIQUES

Collecting vintage watches must not always be in the higher priced sector. There are many interesting brands around with affordable watches for the mass market, also including the bridge technologies between mechanical and quartz.

Timex was amongst the ones setting the pace in this respect (with many others to follow). With the introduction of the electric- and electronic models, the electricity made its way into the watches, which finally led to the quartz watch. The regulating amplitude of these watches was still comparable to the mechanical watches (f = 21,600 A/h = 3.0 Hertz).

With the upcoming of their model 'Q', the quartz crystals finally came along, but at first still restricted to regulating an electro-mechanical movement at an unusual frequency of 49,152 Hertz (normally 32,768). This was a giant step forward.

The tuning fork watches, which have their own chapter later in the book, also getting the power from a battery (Timex did not participate here), went into the same direction, but starting at a higher level. They are already *'humming'* at between 300 and 720 Hertz. Bulova, the inventors of this technique, made their Accutron watches – 'the originals' – swing at 360 Hertz.

But also here, the quartz made it into these watches at a later stage. In the Bulova Accuquartz, a quartz crystal controls a now passive tuning fork, at the standard frequency 32,768 Hertz.

Finally, this was all done away with – the bridge technologies with their hybrid electro- (electronic-) mechanical construction, the quartz controlled electric watches, the watches with active tuning forks, the watches with quartz controlled passive tuning forks. It was all replaced by straightforward quartz watches.

For the collectors however, these bridge technologies are an extremely interesting area. Many people don't even know that electric watches (or tuning fork watches) existed. Some even carried a few of them on the wrist, without really understanding what they had, besides a Timex or one from another manufacturer.

Before we come to the various Timex models, leading us from the mechanical type to the genuine quartz watches, an introduction to the Timex Company itself. They were not only setting the pace with new techniques, but also in new ways of advertising and promotion – with the unforgotten John Cameron Swayze at the front line.

A well assorted Timex collection can show the transition from the mechanical- to the quartz watches, which is a value of its own. Vintage watches made by Timex are *'a dime a dozen'*, in other words cheaply available and still around in large numbers. No wonder: Timex made an incredible number of them – 1,000,000,000 (one billion!) watches between 1950 and 1980 alone, more than 130,000 every working day.

Nevertheless, if you strive to collect their vintage watches only in top condition, not speaking of pristine or NOS, it is ever harder to get your hands on Timex watches meeting these criteria. They have never been watches to collect, but were reliable work horses made for day-to-day use and worn to the very end.

A repair was usually not worthwhile. Most of the movements have cheap pin-lever escapements, without any jewels, simple in their construction, but affordable for everyone. Many of them are still today well running timepieces, if you do not mind a deviation of a few seconds more or less per day. The electric- and electronic watches, which followed the mechanical models, have also simple movements, but provided the most modern technique at the time, some of them even have bearing jewels.

If you want to make a valuation of watchmaking in general, you can look at things under different aspects of appreciation:

- Mechanical watches made by Rolex, Patek Philippe, Vacheron Constantin, Breitling, Lange und Soehne, Omega, just to name a few of the top brands, can be admired for the art of watchmaking, the quality and technique behind.
- Some antique watches, like the chronometers from England, which made a reliable navigation at sea possible, but also other timepieces, have to be seen as masterly achievements of their time, sometimes even changing the course of the world.
- Simple sun dials and scientific discoveries about the heavenly bodies and time have been achievements of advanced civilizations, millenniums ahead of the rest of mankind.
- And then, there are the watches of mass production, simple but reliable companions, steadily performing day after day, affordable for everyone and not just for the rich and privileged.

The latter category was to a lesser extend a question of higher watchmaking craftsmanship, but much more a matter of organized mass production, professional management of large industrial groups, including sales strategies and effective structures.

That this also meant the end of some competitors, unable to keep pace, which either went out of business or had been taken over, often just because of a special technique or a patent, is a different story.

I really don't know what's more fascinating, a watch with numerous complications or the mind-boggling mass of watches made by Timex.

The production of wristwatches under the Timex brand started in the year 1950, with one billion (!) watches made in the following 30 years. That was not always a cozy business. Ups and downs accompanied Timex, who were certainly hit much more by specific developments and events, considering the giant volume of production.

The strike at their plant in Dundee, Scotland, was one of the worst major industrial disputes, notable for its level of picket-line violence, as if Braveheart himself was standing amongst them, fueling the aggressive mood. This has finally led to the closure of the shop, as things took too long and became unbearable (without any judgment about who was wrong and who was right). Even the Scots, in hindsight, were very much surprised by their own courage; there has never been anything like it afterwards.

That was a highly problematic event in 'Dùn Dèagh', as it is called in Scottish-Gaelic. You can't occupy yourself with a lot of things there. It's basically only the three 'J' – jute (textile), jam (marmalade) and journalism. An honorable mention in the category 'jam' should go to the 'Dundonian' (hailing from Dundee) Janet Keiller, inventor of the famous Scottish orange marmalade. Janet came up with the brilliant idea to continually add sugar to cooked bitter oranges, until the compote became edible.

Timex, an 'American business', as they called it, came to Dundee in 1946 and started off with 11 employees in a farm building. At its peak in the early 1970s, that workforce has grown to 7,000 people.

The Timex Company itself was founded in 1854 under the name of Waterbury Clock, Waterbury, in the Naugatuck River Valley, Connecticut, USA, the heartland of the US watch industry in the 19th century.

The sister company, Waterbury Watch, produced the first affordable pocket watch in the year 1880. The wristwatches, produced at a later stage, became highly popular during the WWI period. They were at first small pocket watches. Brackets were added for a canvas strap; the crown was re-positioned to 3 o'clock and hands and numbers were made luminescent – one of the first wristwatches was born.

At the time of WWII, the name of the company was changed to US Time Company and later to Timex Corporation and finally to Timex Group. The latter is still today very active in the watchmaking business with innovative and affordable products.

Timex contributed a lot to the development of the watch industry, yet more in the area of the mass markets. This has been accompanied by an advertising- and sales concept, fundamentally influencing many other producers on the market, not only in the watchmaking business, taking advantage of the latest techniques and the new media.

There are TV commercials which are unforgotten, not just amongst watch collectors. They were produced in large numbers, most of them with the famous host John Cameron Swayze. In these days, the spots were broadcasted live (!) on TV. A special mishap and the smooth mastering of the situation, improvised under live conditions, will be unforgotten in the advertising business as a whole:

In order to demonstrate the water tightness of the Timex watches, a watch was tied to a rotor blade of an outboard motor, rotating in a water tank with 4,500 rpm. After the motor was stopped and lifted up, John Cameron Swayze, who stood by in a rain coat, pointed at the rotor blade to emphasize the intactness of the Timex watch, until he realized that it was not there anymore and slung away from the blade.

At the very moment, he could not immediately find it in the tank, but ensured the viewers, without much hesitation, that this demonstration had gone well during numerous rehearsals before, that he got wet at least six times and that he could confirm the water tightness of the Timex watches.

This TV-commercial also included the famous Timex advertising slogan for their durable watches: *'it takes a licking and keeps on ticking'*.

Above: former TIMEX Museum, Waterbury, Connecticut, USA: cardboard cutout of John Cameron Swayze in his raincoat, with the original requisites of the famous, totally screwed up, but nevertheless smoothly saved live TV-spot, proving the water tightness of Timex watches, attached to a propeller blade of a running outboard motor in a water tank.

The Timex museum was opened in 2001 an old building, erected in the year 1857, the birth house of Timex and in many respects that of modern watches. Unfortunately, it was closed again in the year 2015, because of an insufficient number of visitors. But that is also part of a large industrial group, where history is of lesser interest than the markets of today and tomorrow.

Perhaps it was more due to the location in Waterbury, Connecticut, still today the seat of the company, a place seldom visited by outsiders. In New York City, the number of people per day, just erroneously stumbling upon the museum, would have been higher than that of regulator visitors in Waterbury within a year.

In a similar respect, some brand names in watchmaking (fortunately with more positive examples amongst them) behave not very differently when they come up with a standard answer, following a request for identification of a watch: *'a fire has destroyed all our records'*.

Well, I guess it is up to the collectors to do some of their work and to save not only antique- and vintage watches, but also some technical- and historical facts and information for future generations.

The vintage Timex watches shown on the following pages are sorted in the order mechanical – electric – electronic – quartz controlled electronic – quartz, and a few of a newer date. Timex has not produced any tuning fork watches, most likely as they did not want to work under Bulova license as some other watch companies.

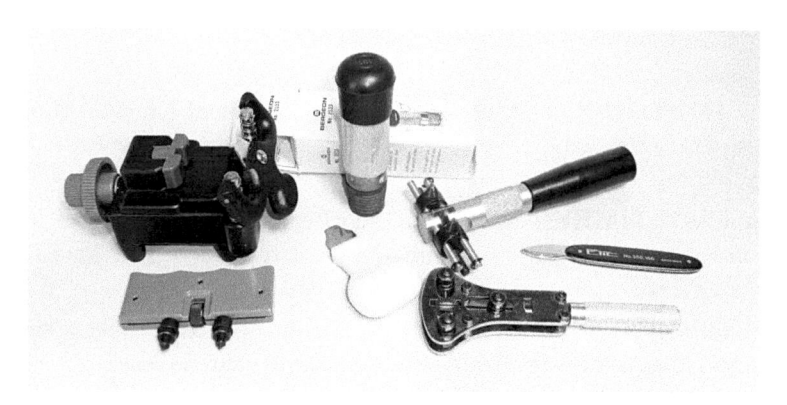

Above: various tools for opening different case backs

TIMEX WATCHES MECHANICAL, HAND WIND

Dating of Timex watches is easy. On most dials, the serial numbers show the year of the making, also the caliber of the movement and other info.

Top left: 1971 TIMEX, USA, gold plated case, movement Timex M24 (no day or date), red dial/white hands, pin lever escapement, no bearing jewels, size (h/v): 39mm x 34mm.

Top right: 1972 TIMEX, USA, gold plated case, movement Timex cal. M25 (with date), pin lever escapement, no bearing jewels, size without lugs (h/v): 33mm x 32mm.

Bottom left: 1977 TIMEX, USA, case chrome plated, stainless steel back, movement Timex M25 (with date), pin lever escapement, no jewels, Ø 34mm.

Bottom right: 1976 Timex, USA, gold plated case, movement Timex cal. M25 (with date), pin lever escapement, no jewels, size without lugs (h/v): 33mm x 30mm.

A watch with day and date in that model range would have a movement cal. M27.

TIMEX WATCHES MECHANICAL, AUTOMATIC

Top left: 1974 TIMEX Automatic, USA, gold plated case, movement Timex M31 (no day or date), pin lever escapement, no bearing jewels, Ø 35mm.

Top right: 1972 TIMEX Automatic, USA, gold plated case, movement Timex cal. M32 (with date), pin lever escapement, no bearing jewels, Ø 35mm.

Bottom left: 1977 TIMEX Automatic, USA, gold plated case, movement Timex M32 (with date), pin lever escapement, no bearing jewels, Ø 35mm.

Bottom right: 1970s TIMEX, USA, case chrome plated, stainless steel back, movement Timex cal. M33 (with day and date), pin lever escapement, no bearing jewels, Ø without lugs 39mm.

TIMEX, 1. ELECTRIC WATCHES, 2. ELECTRONIC WATCHES, 3. QUARTZ CONTROLLED ELECTRIC WATCHES

Watch out mechanical watches, the headsman of the is sharpening the axe!

Well, we know there was a Happy End, so we can follow the next steps fairly relaxed.

With the upcoming of the electric timepieces, the electricity went inside the watches in form of a battery. The initial aim was to replace the mainspring as a power resource with a motor, supplied with electricity by a knob cell. Furthermore, that power was longer available, at the first stage more than a year, instead of winding up the watch after two days the very latest, except for the automatic watches, but also those had certain disadvantages.

The difference between an electric watch and an electronic watch: both are still semi-mechanical, with a more or less conventional balance wheel: An electronic watch has movable electric parts, switches, etc., whereas an electronic watch uses solid state components, like transistors or diodes.

Once it had been recognized that the electricity could also be used for the regulation of the watch, things went unstoppable in a totally new direction.

The quartz controlled electric watch (quartz-controlled balance motor, as also here the rest was still mechanical) finally gave the control over the clocking to a quartz crystal as an electronic oscillator. A similar thing happened with the tuning fork watches. A quartz crystal was regulating the tuning fork, which became a passive element. The regular 'tuning fork watch' is dealt with on page 88 ff.

Finally, all the gap- or bridge technologies came to an end with the appearance of the standard quartz watches as we know them today.

In the year 1959, Timex had acquired Laco – Lacher & Co (watches, founded 1925) and the sister company Durowe (watch movements, founded in 1933), both in Pforzheim, Germany, because the already had an advanced expertise in the area of electric watches. This way, Timex saved time on research and development and, simultaneously, had a direct presence in the growing common European market.

Laco electric watches appeared under their own brand name and then as 'Timex electric made in Germany'. Timex was also producing this type of watches in other places around the world.

Laco/Durowe were sold again by Timex in the year 1965. The company went through a turbulent future thereafter and changed hands several times. However, they managed to pull through and are still around under their present name Laco Uhrenmanufaktur, producing – amongst other models – their famous mechanical pilot's watches.

1. TIMEX ELECTRIC WATCHES

Above left and right: 1960s TIMEX Electric, made in France, stainless steel case, movement Timex cal. M67 (Durowe 861), Ø 34mm. At the beginning there have been some problems with fitting these hybrid electro-mechanical movements into the case, which also needed an accessible place for the battery. The crown, now only needed for setting the time, went to the bottom; quite unusual, like the 'manhole cover' for the knob cell. But soon, the crown went back into the right place and the battery went complete inside and under the back cover, like we know it from a normal quartz watch, and this was certainly more convenient when wearing it on the wrist.

Bottom left: 1969 TIMEX Electric, USA, gold plated case, movement Timex cal. M40 (no date), f = 21,600 A/h, Ø 34mm.
Bottom right: 1970 TIMEX Electric, USA, (identical with the watch on the left), gold plated case, movement Timex cal. M40 (no date), f = 21,600 A/h, Ø 34mm.

85

Above left: 1971 TIMEX Electric, USA, gold plated case, movement Timex cal. M41 (with date), f = 21,600 A/h, Ø 36mm.

Above right: Late 1970s TIMEX Electric Dynabeat, USA, gold plated case, movement Timex cal. M254, f = 28,800 A/h, Ø 34mm.

The Timex Dynabeat must be seen as an attempt to squeeze out the last drop of the idea of electric and electronic watches, whilst the train to the future has already left the station. The normal electric- or electronic watches have a vibrating frequency of 21,600 A/h. This has been raised in the Dynabeat to 28,800 A/h.

2. TIMEX ELECTRONIC WATCHES

Left: 1971 TIMEX Electronic, Germany, made by Laco, gold plated case, movement Timex cal. M85 (date) / Durowe 880, f=21,600 A/h, 3 jewels Ø 42mm.

As mentioned before, this watch differs from the electric types insofar, as movable electric parts, like switches, etc., have been replaced by solid state electronic components, e.g. transistors and diodes. A nice idea is behind the display of the date. It actually switches twice, one day forward with a little dot on top of the date (a.m.) and another short step, to show the dot on the bottom date (p.m.). **See an ad for this watch on the next page.**

Left: 1971 TIMEX ad (watch shown at the bottom of the previous page):

One of the most remarkable things about the Electronic Timex is the price. $50.00.

There are other remarkable things about this remarkable watch. Its transistorized circuit gives you 99.99% accuracy. It never needs winding. A replaceable energy cell gives it power for one year. It has an automatic calendar that keeps you up to date. And a jump sweep second hand that keeps you up to the second. It's water and dust resistant. And comes in a choice of six handsome styles. It's a remarkable watch. At a remarkable price. **The Electronic Timex never needs winding.**

3. TIMEX QUARTZ CONTROLLED ELECTRIC WATCHES

Left: 1972 Timex Q-Quartz, USA, case chrome plated, stainless steel back, movement M63 (with day and date quickset), 2 bearing jewels, balance f = 21,600 A/h, quartz = 49,152 Hertz, size without lugs (h/v): 38mm x 35mm.

This hybrid quartz-electro-mechanical watch is the last step between electric and quartz. The frequency of the quartz is quite unusual. On this watch, the central seconds hand moves 3 times per second.

Over 300 transistors are installed inside the watch within a micro-computer system, which is able to sense and correct any time-keeping variation – thus tuning the watch also to its owner and the way he is wearing the watch. The beat is adjustable through a trim potentiometer.

TUNING FORK WATCHES

The tuning fork watches came along another route, in the end also leading to the normal quartz watches.

The technique has been developed by Max Hetzel, who was working as an engineer for Bulova, Switzerland. The first tuning fork watches under the name Accutron (the name deriving from 'accurate' and 'electronic') were produced by Bulova, but soon other manufacturers followed under their license, like Omega (F 300) or Hamilton with their model Ventura. Not only the shape of the case made the Ventura world famous, it was Elvis Presley, who wore it in the movie Blue Hawaii and also privately.

A Ventura in top condition fetches record prices today. The most famous of the Bulova tuning fork watches, the Space View model, is also in very high demand amongst collectors. It allows a view into the inside of the watch from both sides, consisting mainly of electronic components, soldered wires and plastic parts in gaudy colors, obviously something special in its days.

The tuning fork, which regulates the watch, vibrates at frequencies between 300 and 720 Hertz, depending on the maker and model. For comparison: the concert pitch 'A' has a frequency of 440 Hertz. You can hear the humming sound of the tuning fork when you hold the watch up to your ear.

Announced in 1960, the Bulova Accutron was the first electronic watch which did not need any mechanical balance anymore. The number of needed parts went down to 27, of which 12 moveable. A normal hand wind watch in these days had 136 parts, of which 26 moveable.

Very few watchmakers today are capable of servicing or repairing tuning fork watches (or willing to work on them), which is a risk for a collector. It is also a question of parts and the necessary instruments for testing, tuning and repairing.

Originally, the knob cells used had a voltage of 1.35V, but modern knob cells of 1.5V work fine in most watches. Some particular models need an intermediate part for the cell, dropping the voltage to 1.35V. This does – depending on the construction – not increase the overall size. Lately, new 1.35 Volt know cells are produced again to power delicate instruments, not just watches, highly susceptible to an incorrect voltage. This was made possible, as new material have been found to replace the former cells containing quicksilver.

Compared to the electric- and electronic watches, the vibrating frequency of a tuning fork watch, controlling the clocking, went considerable upwards, about 100 to 200 times.

Electric-/electronic watches, which are hybrid electro-mechanical watches, have a frequency of 21,600 A/h = 3 Hertz, in the range of normal mechanical watches swinging at 2.5 to 5 Hertz. The tuning fork watches 'swing' at 300 to 720 Hertz.

Left and below: 1970 OMEGA F300 Electronic Constellation Chronometer tuning fork watch.

Swiss, movement Omega cal. 1250 (ETA-ESA cal. 9162) serial number 8.0002, gold plated case, hack second (electric), Hesalith crystal with engraved Omega logo in the center, size without lugs (h/v): 38mm x 36mm.

Another fine watch to collect in this area. The number 300 in the F300 stands for its vibrational frequency of 300 Hertz.

On the back of the watch, as usual for the Constellation watches of Omega, the typical engraving with the cupola of the Geneva Observatory and eight stars around in the sky, representing Omegas biggest achievements in precision.

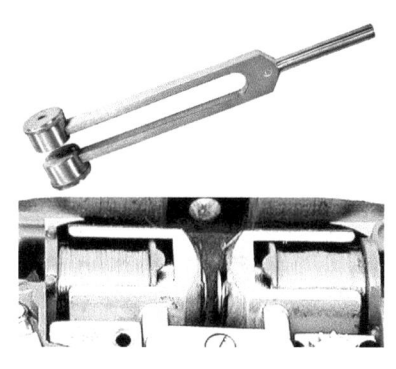

Left, top: Conventional tuning fork

Left, bottom: Tuning fork from a BULOVA Accutron, movement cal. 214.

A conventional watch uses a mainspring as power source and a balance wheel as regulator. The power in the tuning fork watch comes from a button cell. It also supplies electricity to a transistor circuit. The tuning fork is equipped with electromagnets, vibrating at a given frequency.

Some of the movable parts are extremely tiny. A tooth of the ratchet wheel measures 0.025mm (width) and 0.01mm (height). To make this possible, a special material is needed like beryllium copper, which can be milled in such small ranges.

89

The originals: BULOVA Accutron

Bulova's first tuning fork watch was the Accutron, with the movement cal. 214. Many different models of cases have been made. The impressive accuracy, measured against the technological level of the time, was a real quantum leap.

The exploration of the outer space went into new dimensions, and accuracy in timekeeping became much more important. An Accutron watch with a 24-hour dial was used in capsules of the Gemini program. Even the Apollo was equipped with Accutrons.

Many, in these days, went crazy about the Accutrons: 1968, in a German TV show about myths and truth in space exploration, an Accutron was held to a microphone and viewers heard with great excitement the humming noise of the watch, although the sound, similar to that of a tuning fork, should really not be something special as such. I don't want to say that the Roman Emperor Nero had already tuned his harp to that instrument, but correctly leave credit to its inventor, John Shore, who made the first one in the year 1711. He was a Sergeant trumpeter and lutenist to the Royal Court – but that thing in a watch, controlling its clocking – wow!

Above left: 1967 (M7) BULOVA Accutron tuning fork watch, USA, gold plated case, movement Bulova cal. 2180, vibrational frequency 360 Hertz, size (h/v): 34mm x 34mm.

Above right: 1974 (N4) BULOVA Accutron tuning fork watch, USA, gold plated case, grey dial, movement Bulova cal. 2210, vibrational frequency 360 Hertz, size (h/v): 34mm x 35mm.

QUARTZ CONTROLLED TUNING FORK WATCHES

There was also a very last step within the tuning fork technology when the normal quartz watches came along. The **Bulova Accuquartz** now also had a quartz inside (quartz controlled tuning fork), movement cal. 224 family (2240 no date, 2241 date, 2242 day and date), often mixed up with the Accutron Quartz, which is a normal quartz watch. The quartz was controlling the tuning fork, which by then became a passive element. This unusual construction was really coming to the market very late, as Bulova had initially ignored warnings about the upcoming of the cheaper to produce and much more accurate quartz watches. It was a last attempt to come up with something more precise one the basis of the 'old' technology, whilst the future ran away in seven-league boots.

It's an interesting element of this technique that the tuning fork in the cal. 224 is swinging at 341 1/3 Hertz. Now, how can you start with *that* frequency and arrive at increments of a second with an index wheel of 320 teeth (like in the cal. 218)?

In the pure tuning-fork version (cal. 218), we have a vibrational frequency of 360 Hz (vibrations per second) or 360 x 60 x 60 = **1.296.000 per hour**. In the quartz controlled tuning fork (cal. 224), we have a vibrational frequency of 341 1/3 Hz or 341 1/3 x 60 x 60 = **1.228.800 per hour.**

As we need to turn the center wheel and the hour hand around the dial once per hour, and must have a gear train providing the correct reduction.

In a normal quartz watch, the quartz vibrates at 32.768 Hertz (32.768 times per second), which is based on 2 by the power of 15 = 32.768. This is divided by so-called flip-flops (bi-stable multi-vibrator with two stable states - digital divisions by 2), arriving at 1 pulse per second. In the Accuquartz, the quartz inside also vibrates at 32.768 Hertz. It is divided by 32, then by 3, which works out to 341 1/3, the frequency of the regulated tuning fork watch. Yes, and then what, especially as Bulova wanted to use the existing cal. 218 as a basis? You simply change a few teeth in the wheels!

Gear train cal. 218 (wheel teeth/pinions teeth): center 60/10, fourth 56/8, third 54/7, second 45/6, index 320/6.

Gear train cal. 224 (wheel teeth/pinions teeth): center 60/10, fourth 56/8, third 48/7, second 48/6, index 320/6.

Without the center wheel pinion, which is not part of the reduction, the calculations are:

Cal. 218: 60 x 56 x 54 x 45 x 320 = 2.612.736.000 and 8 x 7 x 6 x 6 = 2.016
2.612.736.000 : 2.016 = **1.296.000**

Cal. 224: 60 x 56 x 48 x 48 x 320 = 2.477.260.800 and 8 x 7 x 6 x 6 = 2.016
2.477.260.800 : 2.016 = **1.228.800**

That's the high art of watch engineering, although not attuned to the already fore-seeable developments.

For collectors, interested in the technique of watches, a model Accuquartz is a highly interesting timepiece to have.

Above left: 1974 (N4) BULOVA Accuquartz, quartz controlled tuning fork watch, USA, stainless steel case, movement Bulova 2242 (day and date), vibrational frequency quartz = 32,768 Hertz, vibration frequency tuning fork (passive) = 341 1/3 Hertz, size (h/v): 37mm x 42mm.

Above right: 1973 (N3) BULOVA Accuquartz, quartz controlled tuning fork watch, USA, stainless steel case, movement Bulova 2240 (no date), vibrational frequency quartz = 32,768 Hertz, vibration frequency tuning fork (passive) = 341 1/3 Hertz, size (h/v): 38mm x 42mm. This is the classical version with the divided, differently colored dial and a diamond below the Bulova Accutron tuning fork sign on the left, a model in high demand by collectors.

The quartz controlled tuning fork watch, along with the Timex Q-quartz (a quartz controlled electric watch), marked the end of all bridge technologies between the pure mechanical- and pure quartz-controlled watches, opening the flood gates for the more accurate and much cheaper to produce quartz watches. The initial Tsunami-like wave from the Far East, mostly with lower priced products, brought a severe crisis to the industry of mechanical watches.

Whatever, in a time, where mechanical watches have become obsolete, especially with the radio-controlled models, the mechanical timepieces, together with the old technique, came back like the Phoenix from the ashes, especially in the higher priced sectors. But also the quartz watches have considerably improved their appearance and many well know brand names are also producing in this sector.

In the end, you have to differentiate between two things when judging a technical development. The H4 of John Harrison, the first Chronometer revolutionizing the navigation at sea, was of the finest individual craftsmanship. The quartz technology is also a breathtaking thing if you take a closer look; it's just the end of many technical developments, coming one after another. The developers went from geniuses to well-educated and trained engineers. But also Galileo Galilei's ideas did not come solely from nothing; he also had a basis to work from.

QUARTZ WATCHES

At present (2019), not so many quartz watches make it yet, by age, into the category of vintage timepieces.

Looking at what's already around as vintage from these days, one can observe that very often the ideas went wild with this new and fascinating technique. Every manufacturer wanted to outdo the other, especially as the movements inside became little computers, which could do much more than telling the time, especially when the digital displays came along, with additional indications on the touch of a button.

They are also stopwatches, calculating machines, alarm clocks, date reminders, bio-rhythm calculators, etc.

Funny: despite so much new technique, many of the now vintage pieces have a calendar which already ended many years ago. They didn't even reach into their vintage stage with the calendar still in the time-frame.

The number of moving parts was further reduced, practically down to zero with a digital display, and everything was controlled by a practically indestructible chip.

As quartz watches are well-known instruments to anybody, unlike electronic- or tuning fork watches, the following assembly of examples is just a tiny extract of what's around, without too much information beyond what has already been mentioned before in the book. They are not the prime goal of ambitious watch collectors, although there is a growing community looking also at this area, especially as the first models have come into the age of vintage, and others follow step-by-step.

With the upcoming of the quartz watches and their electronics becoming ever more perfect, manufacturers could also think about replacing the analogue display with LED- (light emitting diodes) and LCD (liquid crystal display) technique.

The eccentric billionaire Howard Hughes, always open to exiting new technologies, participated in the production of these new 'movements' with his company Hughes Aircraft Co., but that had nothing to do anymore with conventional watchmaking.

Hughes was also known for many crazy ideas, like the construction of the largest airplane of the world. The Hughes H-4 Hercules, nicknamed *'Spruce Goose'*, deriving from the material used (spruce) for the body of the aircraft, was such a peculiar inspiration.

The plane never really took off, if you leave aside a few meters above ground on a test flight, but this was at least slightly better than the first flight of a powered airplane in 1903, when Orville Wright took the stick and flew over a beach in North Carolina.

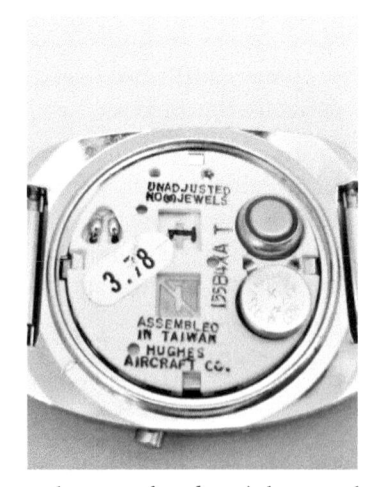

Above left: 1970s TIMEX Quartz LCD, USA, case chrome plated, stainless steel back, with indications of the hours, minutes, seconds, day, date, year and a stop function, size without lugs (h/v): 41mm x 39mm.

Above right: the movement inside this watch, made by Hughes Aircraft Co., assembled in Taiwan.

Above left: the Hughes h4 aircraft in the water. **Above right:** Howard Hughes in the cockpit of this gigantic airplane.

Left: LED display of a TIMEX quartz watch.

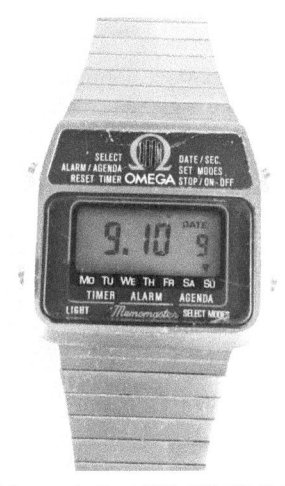

Above left: 1979 OMEGA Memomaster, Swiss, stainless steel case, digital LCD display, multifunction movement Omega cal. 1632, size (h/v): 35mm x 35mm. This was the world's first multi-memory programmable LCD instrument-watch. It is a very rare watch, produced in a total quantity of 19,200 pieces only.

Above right: 1977 BULOVA quartz, USA, stainless steel case, LCD display, day and date shown by push of a button, size (h/v): 40mm x 40mm.

Above left: 1977 BULOVA quartz, USA, stainless steel case, digital LCD display, weekdays indicated on the dial, other indications such as the date upon the push of a button. The movement was made in co-operation with Citizen, size (h/v): 36mm x 40mm.

Above right: 1977 REVUE THOMMEN quartz, Swiss, stainless steel case, digital LCD display, Ø 30mm.

Above left, middle and right: late 1980s TIMEX quartz divers watch, stainless steel, screw down crown, watertight to a depth up to 100 meters (10ATM), direct date set, Ø, round part including bezel: 42mm.

A rather small watch for a diver's model. You can wear this watch under the shower or in the pool, perhaps during some snorkeling. Deep diving would be problematic, as the 10ATM/100 meters are not a professional recommendation. A watch would need a water tightness of at least 20ATM for that purpose. Everything else requires special instruments and not just such a wristwatch, although household divers watches are made up to 100ATM and more. The readability and handleability under water are certainly not comparable with a special instrument.

The bezel on this watch is rotatable bi-directional. Although also highly expensive divers' watches come along in the same way, such a watch or a comparable instrument should have a rotatable bezel only moving counter-clockwise for adequate diving time control. Otherwise, it could lead to an indication of a longer diving time left than actually available, if the bezel is accidentally moved forward; possibly a deadly mistake, which clearly shows that many of the divers watches out there are more a gimmick in the true sense of their alleged function, but certainly held in highest regard amongst collectors.

Left: 1980s FERRARI branded quartz watch, titanium case, red Ferrari dial with the yellow logo, Ø 33mm.

Four very different watches. **Top left and right:** with hour, minutes, seconds, day, date, month and the moon phase. **Bottom, left** with three hands and date. **Bottom, right** with just two hands. Both of the latter would be in the category of a dress watch.

What is a dress watch? The basic requirement: you must feel well when wearing it in a formal (semi-formal) environment and it must easily fit under a shirt sleeve (thin), color yellow gold and round. The things which are more or less open to discussion: diameter between 36mm and 40mm, plain bezel, no numbers on the dial, preferably no date. Some even look at certain straps (and prefer leather) buckle closure, etc., and decide for yourself it must be imperatively mechanical.

Top left to bottom right: **1. CRISTIAN BERNARD, quartz**, France, gold plated case and wristband, day, date, month, moon phase, Ø 32mm.
2. J. CHEVALIER Prestige, quartz, old Swiss brand name – made in Germany, titanium case and wristband, day, date, month, moon phase, Ø 35mm.
3. J. CHEVALIER, quartz, gold plated case and wristband, three hands and date, Ø 33mm. **4. CERTINA, quartz**, Swiss, gold plated, 2 hands only, Ø 33mm.

Above left: 1980s LONGINES, quartz, Swiss, gold plated case, movement Longines L 950.2, Ø without lugs 33mm.

If you want to have the precision and other advantages of a quartz watch without moving to far away from the special flair of a mechanical timepiece, you will also find some renowned watch brands producing quartz watches of higher value, even with their own movements inside. Here, the design and high-quality workmanship all around is well in line with the standards of mechanical watches by Longines.

The hours can be set independently from the minutes (nice for switching to another time zone or to and from daylight savings time). Date quickset in both (!) directions and of course – something more standard – a hack second (the second hands stop for precise and synchronized time setting).

Above right: 1970s BULOVA Accutron quartz, USA, gold plated case, movement Bulova 242 (produced in co-operation with Citizen), size (h/v): 35mm x 40mm.

This watch should not be mixed up with the Bulova Accutron (tuning fork watch), nor with the Bulova Accuquartz (quartz controlled tuning fork watch).

It has a very special feature: with the 'Accuset'-button outside the case at the 4 o'clock position, the time can be synchronized to precise, radio-controlled time signals from another source. If the watch, after a while, is up to 30 seconds fast or slow, the button can be pushed in at the 00-time signal. Then, the motor (and the hands) either runs at double speed until it has caught up, or stops and waits until in line with the correct time.

The chicken feet wristband (newly attached) is certainly a matter of taste, but looks rather nice on this technically interesting and beautiful watch.

Top left: 1980s JUNGHANS quartz ladies' watch, Germany, titanium case, solar powered with rechargeable battery inside, Ø 33mm. Solar powered watches do not only have the normal battery life available to make manual or automatic winding superfluous. The batteries inside are self-recharging, fed by solar power. The durability of these rechargeable batteries is not endless, but certainly a multifold of a normal battery life.

Top right: 1980s PULSAR quartz, USA, stainless steel case, Ø 40mm.

Pulsar came to the market with the first fully electronic watch with LED (light emitting diode) display. At the time, the company belonged to HAMILTON Watch Co., USA. Today, they are today part of the SEIKO Group.

Left: 2016 INVICTA quartz, USA.

'Big is beautiful!' Put next to a men's watch of the 1940s, it would look like a giant on the wrist (and still does without such a comparison).

Stainless steel case Ø 56mm, a height of 18mm and a weight of almost 300 Grams (not even the largest of this brand).

This monster of a wristwatch is certainly not for everybody. Day, date and stop function, screw down crown for better water resistance (100 meters/10 ATM) and a rubber wristband to cope with wet environments.

SWATCH

When you talk about watches on a larger scale, you cannot get around looking at the Swatch group. Their 'Swatch' watches are certainly not in the area of collecting for the aficionado of mechanical timepieces from upper luxury brands, but they also have their fan clubs all over the world, some of them organized in Swatch-Clubs. Especially the early, limited editions still fetch good prices. And what concerns the precision of these watches, they are, like all quartz watches on the whole, superior to any mechanical watch. If you don't believe this, go back to the beginning of the book.

But the Swatch group is a lot more than the Swatch watch. At a certain stage, following the quartz crisis, it looked like *'game over'* for the Swiss watch industry, until a certain Mr. Hayek came along, at first hired by a Swiss government-appointed group, looking at the problems of the watch industry.

Instead of selling out or merging companies, he took a different route. In 1983, he founded a new group, SMH – Société Suisse de Microélectronique et d'Horlogerie, through the merger of ASUAG and SSIH, which both owned a number of well-established Swiss watch brands. Already in control of some famous brands, he put prices up for mechanical watches and emphasized the old label for reliability and first-class craftsmanship 'Swiss Made' or simply 'Swiss'. Luxury goods do not get a better market share by making them cheap; there simply is no cheap luxury. He took over the majority of shares through an investors pool and ultimately became the CEO of the company, which was renamed 'Swatch Group' in the year 1998.

The Swatch group became a worldwide recognized 'shining star' of the watch industry and a model for the revival of an industry, not only in view of watches. Besides coming to the rescue of some Swiss top watchmaking brands, further companies, also outside Switzerland, have been acquired, in addition to the ones already integrated in the group. Parallel to that, the Swatch quartz watches became a big success worldwide and also a watch below this level was produced with the 'Flick Flack' models, helping children to learn time.

Before you eventually make a fool of yourself commenting on the Swatch group: this is the present empire of the most valuable watchmakers in the world:

Luxury segment: Breguet, Blancpain, Glashuette Original, Jaquet Droz, Léon Hatot, Harry Winston, Omega. **Upper segment:** Longines, Rado, Union Glashuette. **Middle segment:** Tissot, Calvin Klein, Bailamin, Certina, Mido, Hamilton. **Basic segment:** Swatch, Flik Flak. **Private label licensing division:** Endura SA.

Also, the movement manufacturer ETA is now part of the Swatch group.

Just a few examples of SWATCH watches, Looka and Smilla from the collector's edition and two others:

Above left: 1996 SWATCH quartz watch, Looka (blue) and Smilla (red) from the collector's edition. They are moving eyes and mouth, which gives their faces a new expression every day. **Above right:** Same watches taken from the body-stand.

Above left: a pair of Looka and Smilla complete with collector's box, papers and collector's pin. **Above right:** 1980s/1990s Swatch quartz watches, a UNICEF edition and a ladies' watch.

Before coming to the radio-controlled watches, a little tribute to the ladies' wristwatches. They are no collector's items in general. Men don't like their size, and mostly they are technically held fairly simple. They sell as vintage watches way below the comparable prices for men's watches, if there should be any interest at all. Women, in turn, are not so much into collecting used items. They are also not particularly interested in wearing the small men's wristwatches from the 1940s or 1950s and usually prefer much larger sizes today.

These are all from NOS (new old stock). The first one (top left) is mechanical, with a new metal wristband. The others (top right also mechanical) came into the collection together with a number of NOS TIMEX men's watches, found in a remote corner of a sunken jeweler store, together with the sales box and papers. Even the batteries in the quartz watches had not leaked after some 20 years inside the watch. Funny how the French differentiate between a quartz watch and a mechanical watch. They call the mechanical watches 'sans pile' (without battery).

Below TIMEX ladies' mechanical watches

Left: 1981, made in Mexico, gold plated, movement Timex cal. M23, size (h/v): 21mm x 21mm.

Right: 1980s, assembled in the Philippines, gold plated, movement Timex cal. M100, Ø with-out lugs 25mm.

Below TIMEX ladies' quartz watches:

Left: 1990s, assembled in the Philippines, gold plated, size (h/v) without lugs 18mm x 23mm.

Right: 1990s, assembled in Thailand, gold plated, Ø without lugs 23mm.

RADIO CONTROLLED WATCHES

The end of the line, what concerns the precision of a watch.

If, one day, there will be mechanical watches with double-tourbillions, self-lubricating bearings, waterproofness below the depth of the Mariana Trench or timepieces equipped with perfume diffusers, automatically scenting farts and spraying through the crown, it can't get any better with a watch in view of correctly telling the time (and much more) – never ever!

Atomic clocks work at a precision of +/- 1 second possible deviation in several million years in long term operations. In short term use, the precision is moving towards 1 billion years before a maximum deviation of +/- 1 second is reached. These clocks, at whatever accuracy, are around since 1949. Of course, you can't have this precision in a wristwatch itself, but you can connect the two.

It was in the year 1967, when Wolfgang Hilbert, at the time working for Telefunken, Germany, filed a patent for the digitally coded time-transmission. Telefunken was involved in wireless communication, producing transmitters and receivers for radiotelegraphy, the radio broadcast and the wireless and cabled transmission technology. All in all, they held over 20.000 patents, were leading in the radar-technology and the inventors of the PAL color television. The company does not exist anymore and the name 'Telefunken', as well as 'AEG', a company they had later merged with, went to a licensing company and the names can now be found on numerous electronic articles of whatever make and quality.

Wolfgang Hilbert was appointed professor at the Darmstadt Technical University, Germany, and developed the first prototypes of radio-controlled watches.

The PTB – Physikalisch Technische Bundesanstalt (Physical Technical Federal Institute), Braunschweig, Germany, has started to transmit time signals in 1973 from an atomic clock, including date, day, month, year and daylight-savings time/winter time via the transmitter DCF77. The transmitter is located in Mainflingen, near Frankfurt am Main, Germany, supplying most of Western Europe. It has a reach of 1500 to 2000 Kilometers. Due to the characteristics of the longwave, overreach distances can go up to Canada, under certain conditions.

Clocks capable of receiving these signals can frequently be adjusted to the precision of an atomic clock. This technique has meanwhile spread over many countries in the world, with different regional transmitters, but still in 1970s just a few radio-controlled clocks had been produced for professional use. In 1986, Telefunken came out with an integrated circuit, enabling the production of cheaper radio-controlled clocks for the mass market.

In 1990, JUNGHANS, Germany, produced the first radio-controlled *wristwatch*, the MEGA1. The antenna was still integrated in the wristband. This had ensured a very good reception, but they were more delicate in daily use on the wrist and replacements were (are) quite expensive. Today, the antennas are inside the watch itself (miniature ferrite rod antenna). If no signal can be received, the watch runs on like a normal quartz watch.

Before that, Wolfgang Hilbert was unsuccessfully trying to persuade the industry to produce radio-controlled wristwatches for everyone. But at the time, cheap and sufficiently accurate quartz watches were flooding the market, bringing the watch industry in a crisis and disorientation. Whatever, shortly after Hilbert's patent had run out, the production of radio-controlled wristwatches finally began.

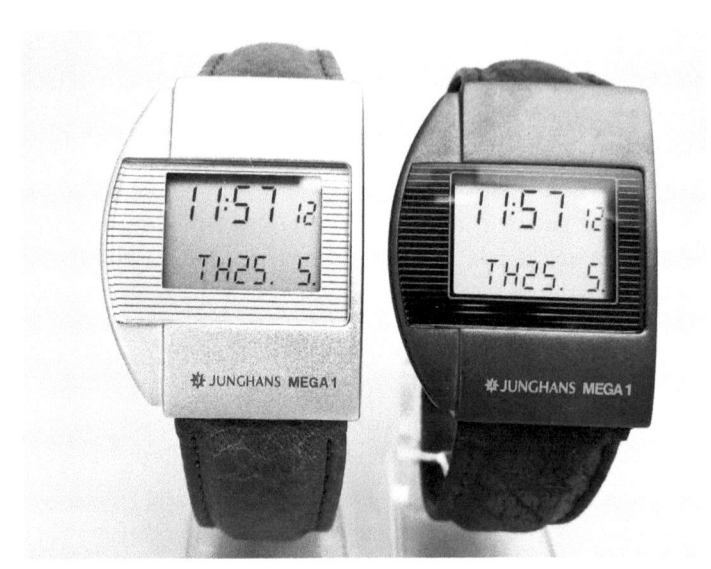

Above: 1990s JUNGHANS radio-controlled watches, the first of that type in the world, spray-painted stainless-steel cases, size (h/v): 33mm x 42mm.

On the left: the MEGA1, model 0010 (26/0010211), made November 1992.

On the right: the MEGA1, model 0013 (26/0013306), made June 1993.

The MEGA1 came out in five different models, 26/0010-11-12-13-14. The last three numbers, which then follow, define year and month of production.

Hours, minutes, seconds, weekday, date, month, with automatic adjustment to summer- (daylight savings) and winter (normal) time.

Have you ever tried to make a picture with two watches of your collection showing exactly the same time, just putting them up as they are?

Junghans, meanwhile under new ownership, still make radio-controlled watches and also (still) supply the market with the old type of antenna-integrated wristbands for the original MEGA1, in a limited number of colors. Of course, there are also many other types of watches in their production line.

Left: 2015 CASIO radio-controlled wristwatch, stainless steel case and wristband. Easy to remove or add links of the bracelet with a small tool contained in the box.

This is an example of what a modern watch can do today, frequently adjusted via radio signal to the precision of an atomic clock.

It features an analogue and digital display, a stopwatch- and alarm function, shows hours, minutes and seconds in analogue display. The digital LCD window can be set to all kinds of indications, stopwatch run down, day, date month, year, alarm times (several). It automatically adjusts to summer- (daylight savings) and winter (normal) time. What's more, it's solar powered with rechargeable batteries. If there is not enough light around, it can go to sleep for several months, reducing functions step-by-step, but continues to go on internally. Battery status indicator, flight mode, etc., etc. With such a radio-controlled watch, you have the time on the wrist with a maximum deviation of +/- 1 second in several million years.

Now, you could say *'who is controlling the possible deviation of +/- 1 second in 1 million (or more) years?'* Well, that's not really an issue. Whatever deviation could possibly exist, it's always the *official* time, and nothing else matters. In any case, the development of time is meticulously followed by the scientists. As a routine measure, the atomic clocks are periodically adjusted with a leap second, not because they would need an adjustment themselves, but due to the change of the time overall in line with the slowing of the Earth's rotation. Via its radio signals, it also corrects the time on the radio-controlled wristwatches.

The MEGA1 has become quite expensive as a vintage collector's item, not so often found in perfect (mint or pristine) condition. The newly produced radio-controlled watches of JUNGHANS are in the higher priced sector. There are makers of good quality in different price ranges like CASIO or CITIZEN, with some others at the more affordable or even cheap end.

Today, we can find the time on a microwave oven, and the makers of radio-controlled watches don't have to get the exact time from an atomic clock. Signals can also be picked up from satellites. The SEIKO Astron GPS Solar uses this new technique, along with solar power; good for globetrotters in remote places and far away from the radio signal of remitting stations. The watch connects by the touch of a button with four or more GPS satellites. Besides picking up the time, they also automatically provide the right local time and a lot of other information. But I'm sure, also this watch will be predominantly worn by people walking around in locations of the civilized world.

ANTIQUE- AND VINTAGE POCKET WATCHES

Also, the watches presented in this section can naturally represent only a half-filled bucket of water from the ocean of different timepieces for the pocket. The selection should nevertheless give a rudimentary overview, focusing on some more basic models and techniques.

The history of watches began in the 16th century. The difference between a clock and a watch (besides size): a clock remains in a stable place, whilst the watch can be carried around. Some languages have just one word for both and need an additional definition to make differentiations, like the term 'Uhr' (clock *or* watch) in German e.g. Tisch*uhr* (table clock), Armband*uhr* (wristwatch).

Where does the English word 'watch' come from? Some believe it derives from old English 'wæcce' (watching, awake, refraining from sleep), itself deriving from the Germanic word 'wakjan' (strong, lively). Others link it to the 17th century, when new time measuring mechanisms were used to determine the length of a watch on board of a ship.

Portable watches evolved from portable spring-driven clocks, which came along already in the 15th century. It was necessary to replace two things before watches could be carried around: The weights as power source (replaced by a mainspring) and the pendulum as regulator (replaced by a rotating balance wheel with a hairspring).

Peter Henlein from Germany was thought to be the inventor of the watch, which was called a clock-watch, worn on the body. If he was really the first or someone else, is still discussed amongst the experts. The first timepieces were made in Nuremberg and Augsburg, Germany, in the early 16th century, in size somewhere between a small clock and a pocket watch of today. It was attached to the clothing or worn on a chain around the neck. In these days, the accuracy of these watches was close to useless and a look around or to the sky gave a better indication of the time of day. They were primarily a piece of 'living jewelry', which had to be wound up more than once a day.

English and French watchmakers, amongst others, laid the grounds for many steps ahead with revolutionary inventions. Individual watchmaking, step-by-step, made room for industrial production and finally the mass production around the mid of the 19th century. Of course, there was the Swiss watch industry, becoming the most important in the world, whilst in the USA, the mass production climbed to ever new heights.

The development went on, up to complicated and very precise timepieces, with numerous improvements, convenient to handle and wear. Pocket watches, attached to leather straps, were the first watches carried on the wrist around the early 20th century, until the wristwatches, as we know them today, took their own path.

Early pocket watches were based on a verge escapement and a fusee/chain combination. They were wound up and set with a small key. The power is transmitted from the spring via a chain onto a cone-shaped fusee. The weakening of the power of the main spring, especially as the material was not as good as in later times, was compensated by the increasing leveraging effect, as the chain went down on the fusee. The key was later replaced with a winding crown, as we see it on later pocket watches.

Left: watch keys, top = new, **middle** = old, **bottom** = watch chain with a pendant (chatelaine).

Key wind pocket watches can seldom be found with the original key(s). They have been lost, were damaged or were sold separately. Fine specimens, especially set with precious stones or elaborately designed, are very much wanted items, occasionally even more valuable than the watch it belonged to.

New keys are available in various sizes and in different qualities, fitting well, or not so well, on the square shafts for winding and setting. There is, however, a problem with new keys which are made of steel-material as available today. The square shafts on the watches for winding and setting are made of iron, relatively soft compared to today's steels. This is often a reason for damaging the shaft with a key that does not fit correctly.

Watch chains or pendants (chatelaines), like the ones shown on the bottom, are also much sought after by collectors.

Below: verge escapement.

This escapement is installed in a large clock, at display at the Deutsches Uhrenmuseum (German watch- and clock museum), situated near Furtwangen in the Black Forest, an historic center of watch-making.

The verge escapements in the old pocket watches, a lot smaller of course, are of the same construction.

Silver Hallmarks: When an item made of silver was to be sold commercially, many countries had them stamped with one or more marks, besides setting certain standards. There are countries like Germany, Russia and others, where not only the purity of the material is indicated, but also other relevant information about maker, place of production, etc. The British hallmarking system is one of the best, if not *the* best in the world. Lots of information can be taken from those marks, making collecting silver items from that area not only very interesting but also more transparent, for dealers and collectors alike – not to speak of the superior quality and craftsmanship.

A typical set of hallmarks in English sterling silver watches (and not only there) would be: 1. standard of purity (material) 2. city mark 3. date letter (year of manufacture) 4. duty mark and 5. maker's mark (case, pendant).

This takes out all guessing about the age of a watch, and provides also other valuable information. Very often, especially on older watches made before the industrial production came along, we can find the name of the watchmaker on the dial. There are some fantastic books available, supporting the research and giving much other valuable information. The books shown on the image below are amongst the 'must-haves' for any serious collector: 1. The latest edition of 'Watchmakers and Clockmakers of the World, Brian Loomes 2. Bradbury's Book of Hallmarks 3. English Silver Hallmarks, edited by Judith Banister 4. Watch Case Makers of England, Philip T. Priestley.

Above (all images): small verge fusee pocket watch, approx. 1785, Carré, Geneve (Geneva), Switzerland, verge escapement, power transmission via chain and fusee, enameled dial, double case fire gilded silver, key wind (back) and key set (front, at the center arbor), movement èbauche (raw movement without case, dial and hands) from the Royal Manufacture, Ferney (near Geneva), Ø 41mm.

There are several watchmakers by the name of Carré in France, as well as in Switzerland, who would fit into the time frame. The maker of this watch was most likely Swiss or working in the French part of Switzerland. The movement has a so called 'potence', an adjustable bracket for the verge escapement, invented by the French watchmaker Julien LeRoy around 1730. The design was changed in the middle of the 18th century and became a defining feature of the French-Swiss design. After 1800, this was abandoned again.

Above (all images): verge fusee pocket watch, England, between 1750 and 1780, watchmaker John Josephson, London, verge escapement, Tompion regulator, power transmission via chain and fusee, enameled dial, double case silver fire gilded, key wind (back) and set (front, at the center arbor), Ø 50mm.

Above (all images): verge fusee pocket watch, England, between 1750 and 1780, watchmaker John Richard, London, verge escapement, power transmission via chain and fusee, enameled dial, double case fire gilded brass, key wind (back) and set (front, at the center arbor), large diamond center stone, Ø 50mm.

In the outer double housing, which serves as an additional protection for the watch, there is a paper inlay of a watchmaker and jeweler John Watt, 7 Duke Street, Huntly, Scotland, where the watch has either been originally sold or, at a later stage, brought in for service or repair. The shop is gone, but the old house is still there and occupied by another business.

Further to the watch on the page 110: When the watchmaker John Richard from London made this watch, Wolfgang Amadeus Mozart had just completed his Coronation Mass and was beginning to work on his opera Idomeno.

It was also around the at time of the American War of Independence (1775-1783). The watch is still today running well and precise within its limits.

Mozart with sister Anna and father Leopold, with a portrait of his mother on the wall, who died unexpectedly in 1778 in Paris on a trip together with Mozart in search of a better employment.

Writing the Declaration of Independence, 1776

Thomas Jefferson (right), Benjamin Franklin (left), and John Adams (center) meet at Jefferson's lodgings on the corner of Seventh and High (Market) streets in Philadelphia, to review a draft of the Declaration of Independence.

Above (all images): verge fusee pocket watch, Swiss, between 1780 and 1799, verge escapement, power transmission via chain and fusee, enamel dial, double case brass 9K fire gilded, key wind (back) and set (front, at the center arbor), Ø 50mm. Coulin was a Swiss watchmaker working in Geneva at the end of the 18th century.

The watch, today a rare piece, was at the time produced more for the upper middle class and those of them who could afford it.

The watch needed a new crystal and a fitting and one could be found from the time, which is not so easy. These crystals need to be of the high dome type, with a strong curvature in the middle, providing sufficient room over the high square shaft where the time is set.

The movement has a balance bridge (screwed down at both ends) unlike a balance cock (held in place just at one end) – see next watches on page 113 and page 114.

Above (all images): sterling silver verge fusee pocket watch, England, 1797, watchmaker Walter (Watt) Heasman. Lindfield (Sussex), born 1748, enameled dial, **case maker: Thomas Carpenter**, 5 Islington Road, London, has later moved up to 9 Islington Road.

Hallmarks: sterling silver (0.925), London, date letter for 1797. Duty mark: The sovereigns head, in use between 1775 and 1806, Ø 55mm.

The watch must have been made for a special person. Instead of the numbers from 1 to 12, the letters (name) E-D-W-A-R-D C-A-R-T-E-R can be found on the dial.

An inlay in the case, with a handwritten note, comes from William Dann, watch & clockmaker and jeweler, Maidstone, Kent, who had serviced or repaired this watch for a 'Mister Carter', perhaps the original owner or a relative.

Moving forward to the first half of the 19th century. The verge escapement has meanwhile largely been replaced by a pointed tooth escapement, and an indication for the seconds has been implemented.

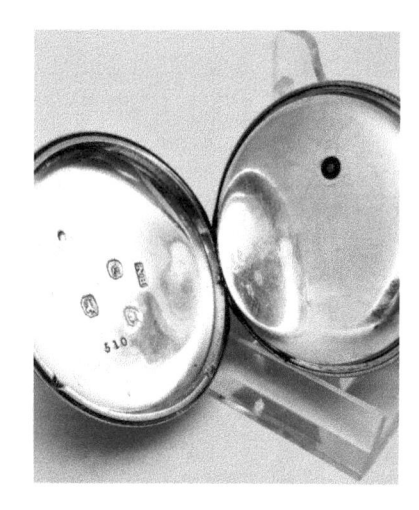

Above (all images): 1836, sterling silver pocket watch, England, watchmaker Thomas Strange, Banbury. Case maker Benjamin Norton (initials 'B.N.'), Banner Street, St. Luke's (London), registered his business in 1824. Enameled dial, pointed tooth escapement, power transmission via chain and fusee, diamond center stone, key wind (back) and key set (front, at the center arbor), seconds indication (decentral), spring lid (back).

Hallmarks: sterling silver, London, date letter 1836, Ø 46mm.

Above (all images): 1848 sterling silver pocket watch, England, watchmaker Charles Yeomans, Hull. Case maker William Fielder.

Very similar watch to the one on the preceding page 114. It also has the new pointed tooth escapement, the indication of the seconds (decentral), but now also an additional protective cover inside.

Enameled dial, pointed tooth escapement, additional protective cover inside, power transmission via chain and fusee, key wind (back) and key set (front, at the center arbor), seconds indication (decentral), spring lid (back), Ø 50mm.

Hallmarks: sterling silver, London, date letter 1848.

Moving on to the second half of the 19th century:

Below (all images): **MI Chronometre, most likely Swiss, approx. 1860**, brass case, enameled dial, sawn plate, built in compass. Key wind and key set are now both done from the back. The cylinder escapement inside was already invented in 1695 in England by Tomas Tompion, but it was never really popular there and ceased completely after the lever escapements had been perfected in the early 19th century, Ø 53mm.

This watch is a bit out of the ordinary. Some collectors will throw their hands up in horror, others might simply find it 'interesting'. In any case, this timepiece is a good example showing us that phony watches appeared on the markets long before the faking of luxury brands.

The watch boasts with features it doesn't have. The large engraving 'MI-Chronomètre' (French for chronometer), is a false and misleading labeling, combined with a 'MI', on a nice watch for common people. A chronograph would be a very precise, high grade watch and needs to be certified as such. This term, widely known as a quality label, was often falsely used to attract buyers. Today, this designation is officially protected (at least in our parts of the world). Since 1973 we have the COSC – Contrôle Officiel Suisse des Chronomètres, Switzerland. Although this is a purely Swiss institution for voluntarily self-regulation, leading- and renowned manufacturers from many countries are obtaining their certificates from the COSC.

The number of allegedly installed 22 jewels is totally exaggerated. The nicely sawn plates were most likely made in home-based work, when peasants and farmers occupied themselves during the winter months with making watch components. The compass built in is certainly an attraction and works well, like the watch itself.

Above (all images): 1866 silver pocket watch, England, watchmaker Henry Foster, Liverpool, case maker George Richards, London.

The pendant was usually produced separately from the case, maker here: James Jackson, London.

Enameled dial, pointed tooth escapement, additional protective cover inside, power transmission via chain and fusee, key wind (back) and key set (front, at the center arbor), seconds indication (decentral), Ø 46mm.

Hallmarks: sterling silver, Birmingham, date letter 1866.

Above and below (all images): 1876 silver pocket watch, England, enameled dial, pointed tooth escapement, power transmission via chain and fusee, key wind (back) and key set (front, at the center arbor), seconds indication (decentral). The watch does not only have a second housing outside, but also a protective cover inside the watch. The jewel for the bearing of the balance shaft is held in a 'chaton' (a circular piece of metal holding the ruby which is used as bearing of the pin/pivot or shaft). This can either be pressed in or is, like in this watch, fixed by three screws, which is a higher-grade constructional design, Ø 51mm.

Hallmarks: sterling silver, London, date letter 1876.

Also, the initials 'H.B.' can be found. They belong to the case maker Henry Buckland, Moat Street (later Spoon Street), Coventry, where he worked from 1853 to 1867 and later, under a new logo, from 1868 to 1879.

There is no name of a watchmaker on the dial. Watchmaking has already moved farther down the road towards industrial production.

As this was becoming less and less individual work, no specific name was added any more to average- and standard products.

Above and below (all images): 1877 silver pocket watch, England, verge escapement, enameled dial, power transmission via chain and fusee, key wind (back) and key set (front, at the center arbor), seconds indication (decentral), Ø 50mm. The second outer housing is unfortunately missing on this watch. Hallmarks: sterling silver, London, date letter 1877. This date letter is somewhat of a surprise, because of the verge escarpment inside the watch. Since some time, this had already been replaced by the pin-lever escapement and can only very seldom be seen after 1850. Perhaps, someone has made use of the last old parts left in stock.

There are fine hair cracks on the dial. When you look at those cracks, you actually do not see the crack itself, but the dust and dirt which have settled within.

With the right method, this can be nicely cleaned. The crack is not gone, but only hardly visible thereafter.

Also here, no watchmaker left his name on the movement, as it was becoming common practice versus the period of industrial production. No case maker can be identified, but the maker of the pendant, which was usually produced separately.

The initials 'W.S.' stand for William Skidmore, 22 Brewer Street, Goswell Road, London. With the round pillars and the Bosley-regulation of the movement, it must be one of the very last specimens with a verge escapement.

The movement of this watch has a wonderful balance cock with a grim face. This can be seen quite often and symbolizes the north wind.

Above and below: open face pocket watch, France, approx. 1880, movement Japy 16" (Japy Freres 16 lines), enameled dial, cylinder escapement, key wind and set in the back, monometallic balance wheel, case marked 'Argentan', Ø 50mm. Argentan (colloquially called nickel silver) is an alloy of nickel, copper and zinc. The designation Argentan is intentionally misleading, suggesting a silver content based on the Latin word 'argentum' (silver), but has nothing to do with it. The combination of a cylinder escapement and key wind and key set is nothing so unusual as, unlike in England, this type of escapement was more popular in other countries. It was used in affordable watches for a long time to come, even later, when the winding was done with a crown. The watch, an example of earlier mass production, has been made by Japy Freres, Beaucourt, France in the late 19th century. Their logo 'Beaucourt' appears both on the watch and on the case.

Japy Freres, founded in 1773, was one of the pioneers of mass production. They extended their product range to pumps (still making them today), agricultural equipment (until 1941), combustion engines, gas, oil, gasoline or alcohol (until 1941), household appliances, photo cameras or typewriters (until 1972) metal drinking cups and plates for the army as well as steel helmets. The production of watches has since long been given up. The production of motors finally went to Renault. There is also a strong connection to Peugeot, another large car manufacturer in France. At some stage, there had been efforts to re-activate Japy as a watch brand. At first Matra Horologerie took over and wanted to combine Japy with other brands like Jaz and Yema. Japy was subsequently sold, together with Yema to Seiko. In the year 1996, Jaen-Paul Suchel obtained the rights on Japy again. In the same year, their new generation diver watches came out, but soon, the vision of Jean-Paul Suchel ended with the final discontinuation of production.

Above (all images): open face pocket watch, Swiss, 1880-1890, case nickel, cylinder escapement, key wind and key set (both in the back), sawn movement plate, Ø 48mm. The dial is richly decorated and painted. The back has been engraved with a rural motive, perhaps aiming at this target group of customers, but these motifs have been popular in general. The movement is quite simple, but impresses with its sawn plates, which had mostly been produced by peasants and others in home-based work during the wintertime.

The Swiss also used the cylinder escapement in these days. The marking 'Cylindre' (cylinder) comes in oversized letters, although nothing very special, even in those days. Around the same time, the typical Swiss lever escapement emerged in Germany at the end of the 19th and the beginning of the 20th century. It was a further development from the 'Glashuette lever escapement'. At first, it was called 'Kolbenzahn-Ankerhemmung' (club tooth escapement). As all watches in Switzerland had subsequently been produced with this type of escapement, with frequent improvements, the name Swiss lever escapement became the widely used term.

Above and left: open face pocket watch, approx. 1890, Swiss, lever escapement, enameled dial, case nickel silver-coated, key wind and key set (both in the back), Ø 46mm.

The movement has a special feature, a counter-weight at the anchor, to provide a more even and balanced movement of the anchor (see image on the left, the curved part with a heavier tip).

Left: watchmaker's lathe shown in a 1899 catalogue.

Left and below (all images): large and heavy open face pocket watch, England 1897, sterling silver, enameled dial, pointed tooth escapement, decentral seconds, key wind (back) and key set (front, at center arbor), spring mechanism back lid, weight 170 grams, Ø 60mm.

The watch was designed to be a durable and reliable timekeeper. The time must still be set at the front at the center arbor, which is a technique that was already made obsolete by the watches which have a second hole in the back, to make time settings through a mechanism in the movement.

The balance is still of a simple, non-bi metallic type, without any screws. No watchmaker engraved, case maker: George Hammon, Coventry, who registered his business in 1881. Works from him are known from 1884 to 1896. This must therefore be one of the last cases made by him.

Hallmarks: sterling silver, Birmingham with date letter 1897. Pendant (separately made) marked: London, date letter 1897.

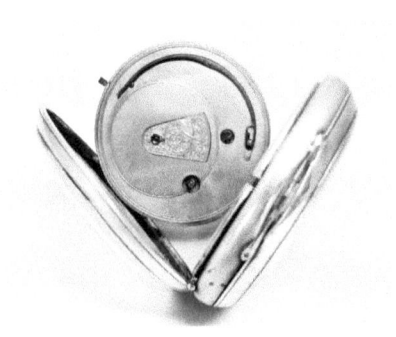

Page 124 and 125 (all images): sterling silver open face pocket watch, England, 1897.

The images on next two pages give a good impression of the construction of this particular pocket watch and its hallmarking.

It has the following features: **single outer case, fold away crystal to access the center arbor for setting the watch, fold away dial to get inside, additional protective cover, foldable back lid to get to the square shaft for winding; the movement cannot be accessed from this side.** Pointed tooth escapement, key wind (back) and key set (front, at the center arbor), power transmission via chain and fusee, compensating balance and screw balance, dial with nice chasing, Ø 55mm.

Hallmarks: sterling silver (lion), city of Chester with date letter 1897.

Here, the watchmakers have engraved their name on the movement. In most watches, from the beginning of the industrial production onwards, this cannot be seen anymore, especially in simple and affordable models. This watch however, and especially the movement, is of higher value and better technical standards.

Watchmaker(s), as engraved on the movement: John Hewitt and Son, London.

The case was made by James McKnight (initials J.M.K.), Coventry. There are also hallmarks on the pendant, which was usually made by someone else, showing the lion for sterling silver, the city mark for Birmingham and the date letter 1896.

Before moving forward to the first half of the 20th century, a few watches from an interesting watch company, made around that period (the production already started in the 19th century). Their watches are, in several respects, ideal candidates for a collection. Of course, there are other watchmaking companies with a similar background.

Pocket watches (and wristwatches) made by **Waltham**, formerly called American Waltham Watch Co. or American Watch Co., are in high regard amongst collectors. This is, on one hand, due to the good quality, up to the 'railroad grade' pocket watches, used also by American railroad companies, and which needed to be approved and certified as such. On the other hand, Waltham is providing most extensive information for owners and collectors about all important details of a watch, simply by the serial number on the movement. This is seldom matched to that extend by other producers. No guessing around, like with many of the other brands, for instance when trying to determine the exact production date.

All watches, including those intended for general use, are of high quality, sturdy and mostly of them fairly heavy. The movements are usually embellished with nice engravings.

Waltham did not only make complete watches, but was sending also raw movements around the world. They are much sought after by collectors if they are still in the original tin transport-boxes.

Waltham watch factory, view from around 1930

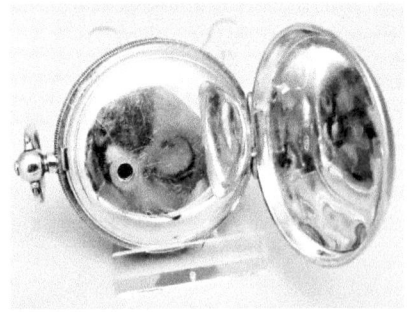

Above (all images): **WALTHAM – A.W.W, Co. / American Waltham Watch Co.**, serial number 9364567, sterling silver open face pocket watch, USA/England 1899/1901 (movement model 1883), lever escapement, bi-metallic compensating balance/screw balance, key wind (back) and key set (front, at the center-arbor), decentral seconds indication, 7 jewels, Breguet spiral, movement finish gilt, Ø 51mm.

Only the movement of this watch was exported to England. Based on the serial number, we know that it was produced in the year 1899. The prototype had been completed in 1883, with the production starting in 1885. The total production, from 1885 to 1919 was 941,872 pieces.

The case was made by the Dennison Watch Case Company. The hallmarks (case and pendant) indicate sterling silver and Birmingham with date letter 1901. The initials 'A.B.' belong to Alfred Bedford, director of Waltham in Great Britain. He was linked to Aaron Dennison, who left Waltham in 1862 and went to England to set up a watch case manufacturing company (Dennison Watch Case Company). As the separation from Waltham was not so harmonious, Waltham did not want to see his name on the English made cases of Waltham watches and resorted to the name of Alfred Bedford and his initials.

Above (all images): WALTHAM open face pocket watch from 1904, USA, sterling silver, lever escapement, compensating balance / screw balance, 7 jewels, Breguet spiral, **winding and setting already via the crown**, screw-on bottom lid, Ø 50mm.

The watch is a model 'Traveler', in simpler construction. It has a solid screw-on back lid, which has, in a lot of cases, lead to severe damaging, when collectors wanted to pray open the watch, as this is usually done on snap-on back-covers. Movement serial number 14097799: model 1899, production year 1904, total production between 1899 and 1908 = 286,550 pieces.

The silver hallmarks inside the back lid are very interesting. They show the German 'Reichskrone' (imperial crown) according to the hallmarking law of 1884. Shortly before, 39 still independent German states have founded the German Nation (1871). The case, further processed by the Philadelphia Watch Company, USA, has therefore been imported from Germany into the USA. Sterling indicates a silver fineness of 0.925. Movement finish = nickel. This model came in gilt (gold plated) and nickel. Nickel was used in later years, especially in expensive watches, because of its greater durability and better characteristics for engraving.

Left and below: WALTHAM open face pocket watch, USA 1908, model 1899, enameled dial, compensating balance-wheel / screw balance, lever escapement, 7 jewels, Breguet spiral, decentral seconds indication, winding and setting via the crown, double snap- on back covers, Ø 51mm.

Another model 'Traveler' for day-to-day use. Total production of that model between 1899 and 1908 = 286,550 pieces.

The movement finish is nickel; the case was made by Illinois Watch Case Co., Chicago, Illinois.

Above: Mainspring and barrel of a small alarm clock. The construction, in such a simple version, is basically the same in a pocket- or wristwatch.

Watches coming up: first half of the 20th century.

Above left and right: open face pocket watch, Equity Watch Co., Boston, USA, approx. 1911 to 1917, lever escapement, winding and setting via the crown (= stem wind and –set), bi-metallic compensating balance wheel/screw balance, Breguet spring, enameled dial. Both the front bezel with the crystal, as well as the back lid are screw-on. This is often the reason for defects beyond repair, as some collectors try to pry open the lid before realizing it's a screw-on type, Ø 51mm.

The case was made by the Wadsworth Watch Case Company, Newport, Kentucky. **Equity Watch Co. was a company of Waltham Watch Co.**, making affordable watches of nevertheless good quality.

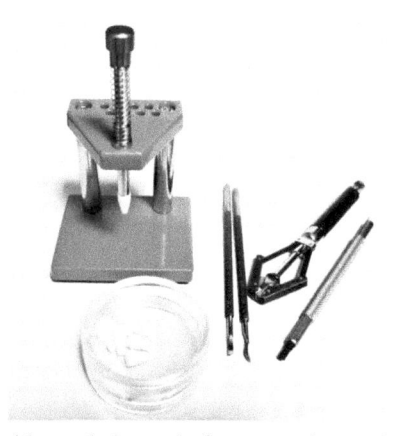

Above left: tools for removing and setting hands. **Above right:** watchmaker's parts cabinet filled with different crowns.

Above and left (all images): open face chronograph pocket watch, Swiss, Le Phare, approximately 1910 to 1920.

Gun metal case, enameled dial, movement Le Phare cal. 114 VCC, lever escapement, Breguet balance (Breguet hair spring). Screw balance (not compensating), winding and setting via the crown, stop watch function with push button in the crown. Chrono-function 60 seconds-, 30 minutes- recording, decentral seconds indication, Ø 52mm.

The 144 VCC is the most famous movement of Le Phare, Le Locle, Switzerland. These watches, also called 'navigation timer', came with a gun metal case and had been made especially for the military. In WWI, not only the pilots of the German Luftwaffe flew around with it, but also those of the French Armée de l'Air. It could also be found amongst American pilots. Before the USA officially entered the war, some of their pilots had already been flying for the French air force.

This reliable movement, highly regarded in its time, was also installed in other watches. Le Phare (French for lighthouse) was founded in 1888 by Charles Barbezot and was temporarily taken over by Zenith (1915) and became independent again in 1922. Founder of Zenith (or rather their predecessor company) was the famous Swiss watchmaker and entrepreneur George Favre-Jacot. Zenith is still around as manufacturer of expensive, high grade watches.

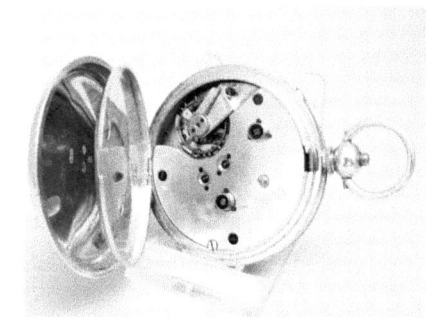

Above (all images): sterling silver open face pocket watch, England 1919, enameled dial, pointed tooth escapement, bi-metallic compensating balance wheel/screw balance, key wind and set (both in the back), central seconds hand, Ø 56mm.

The watch is quite large and heavy (approx. 130 grams). The back lid has a spring mechanism, which is released by the button in the pendant.

The watch is still key wind and –set (both in the back), but already has a central seconds indication. Around the dial, the graduations of the segments for the seconds go up to 300, each representing 1/5th of a second (60 x 5 = 300). This is not just a nice gimmick, imitating a 0-300 scale, a classic feature on English navigation chronographs. The seconds hand really moves around in 1/5th of a second increments, which requests a special toothing in the gear train.

Hallmarks: case sterling silver, imported into England (English import mark), London with date letter 1919. The initials 'W&H' belong to Wills & Hill, importers of watch cases, Mark Lane, London, registered 1918.

Left: 1920s OMEGA pocket watch, rare 24-hour day-night dial with cardinal points, case silver 0.800, lever escapement, movement Omega 19LB SIBN, decentral seconds indication, winding and setting via the crown, Ø 58mm.

The hour hand goes around in 24 hours and not in 12 (2 x 12). This requests a different gearing of the hour hand. The time indications from 13:00 to 24:00 have additional numbers underneath, following the 1 p.m. to 12 p.m. systematology.

Additionally, the enameled dial itself, difficult to see on the image, is horizontally divided into a white upper part and a greyish part below, for the periods of day- and nighttime.

With the hour hand going around the dial in 24 hours instead of 12, reading the time – and to know if it's a.m. or p.m. – is made very clear, perhaps a good thing if that is not so easy to determine in a place without daylight or in certain remote locations of the world with several months of continuous days and nights.

Left: OMEGA advertisement of 1923.

The watch of precision, OMEGA, constantly gives the exact time. On sale at all concessionary horologists and at Kirby, Beard & Co., Paris, 5 rue Auber.

Left and below (all images): open face pocket watch, Swiss, 1920 to 1925, Galli, Zurich

Movement Longines cal. 19.75, lever escapement, bimetallic balance/screw balance, Breguet hairspring, decentral seconds indication, stem- (crown) wind, Swiss Patent 16831: two-section regulator for coarse and fine adjustment, filed Feb. 15, 1899, by Charles Brisebard, Besançon, France, enameled dial, gun metal case, made for and sold by Galli, Zurich, Ø 50mm.

When setting the time, the crown is not pulled out, but stays in its position. A little pin is pressed in for this purpose, outside on the case at the 1 o'clock position, then the crown is turned as usual (stem/pin-set system). The case is made from iron (gun metal), a material often used during economical difficult times.

The origins of Galli Uhren Bijouterie (watches and jewelry) AG, Zurich, reach back into the 19th century.

'Galli hat Zeit – seit 125 Jahren' (Galli has time – since 125 years) is their slogan and also a unique and clever wordplay. It can mean both in German, 'having time', in a sense of not being in a hurry, but also 'having the time' in relation to the horological products they are selling.

Seeking help to determine the age of the watch, Galli in Zurich had been contacted, along with a few images and the statement that the watch had recently been acquired at an auction.

The answer came promptly, explaining that these watches were sold in the years 1920 until 1925 – almost 100 years ago. Chapeau! Certainly different from the standard answer one will too often obtain from many, even prominent, watchmakers and sellers, who claim that all documents had unfortunately been destroyed by a fire, etc. – occasionally an easy way out of getting involved in 'unproductive' work.

Above (left and right): small ladies' half-hunter double dial pocket watch for a necklace, early 20th century, cylinder escapement, silver gilt case, stem (crown) wind and set, Ø 37mm. Savonette (hunter) watches have the crown at the 3 o'clock position and are viewed from the side, taking into consideration their attachment on a chain; the same applies to larger hunter men's watches, carried on a watch chain.

Above (left and right): pocket watch OMEGA 1935/1936, serial number 8.202.411, case stainless steel chromium plated, lever escapement, movement OMEGA cal. 38.5L T1, 15 jewels, bi-metallic compensating balance / screw balance, decentral seconds indication, stem (crown) wind and set, Ø 47mm.

The watch has an unusual lift angle of 38°. The angle needs to be known when determining the balance wheel's amplitude. Normally, it is closer to 52°, mostly set as default for timegraphers when the lift angle is not known. Omega can take pride in making superior products, but they are offering also an outstanding service when it comes to documentation and related information. The angle was obtained directly from Omega within a couple of days — for a product they sold 80 years ago, and which went through who knows how many hands in the meantime.

Above (left and right): full hunter pocket watch, France 1940. A full hunter has a protective cover at the front, the half hunter is an open type. Both have the crown at the 3 o'clock position.

The lid at the front is released by a button in the crown. Gold plated, lever escapement, decentral seconds, movement HP – Fabrique d'Ebauches (raw movements) H. Parrenin, France, closed monometallic balance wheel (monometallic), but with screws = screw balance, Breguet spring, Ø 45mm.

Difficult to say who has made this watch. The case is marked 'Bréguet watch case importe de Suisse' (watch case imported *from* Switzerland), case makers Bréguet Watch Case, André Bréguet SA, Biel, Switzerland. The initials JBB stand for J. Bréguet-Breting.

The designation 'Chronometre' (chronometer) on the dial is just for marketing purposes and not a quality mark for a genuine and certified chronometer. The term was often misused, as it was not adequately protected in these days and common people did not have the relevant knowledge.

The 'prime time' of pocket watches is coming to an end over the next years.
These watches are still made into our days, but compared to the competition of the wristwatches, the market share of new pocket watches sold is step-by-step becoming smaller and smaller, down to a wallflower existence.

Pocket watches held on to their dominant presence a lot longer at first, as wristwatches did not have a large general acceptance. The latter were not considered to be 'real watches', especially at the beginning, until a big push came during and after WWI, when the military ordered wristwatches in larger quantities.

Moving on to the second half of the 20th century:

Above (left and right): 1950s open face pocket watch, KIENZLE, Germany, stainless steel, movement Kienzle cal. 46, pin lever escapement, monometallic balance wheel, stem (crown) wind and –set, decentral seconds indication, Ø 50mm. This was a simple watch, as most people could afford following the years after WWII, without any shock protection or bearing jewels. Nevertheless, it was a very reliable companion for many people, sturdy and durable for deades. The luminous material on the dial and hands contains radium – see also chapter 'Radium contamination' on page 30.

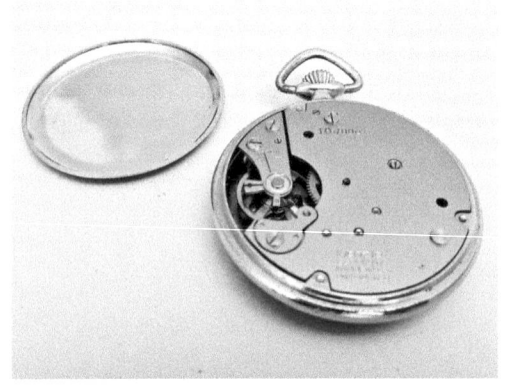

Above (left and right): 1960s open face pocket watch, KIENZLE, Germany, stainless steel, movement Kienzle cal. 146/00e, pin lever escapement, monometallic balance wheel, stem (crown) wind and –set, decentral seconds indication, Ø 50mm.

Not much different from the watch on the top. The concept of making simple, affordable, yet very reliable watches for the emerging mass market, has proved successful. It seems, that the luminous material on the dial and hands still contains radium (Geiger counter measurement), although we have come to the time where this was already replaced by the more harmless tritium.

Although not in 'high' demand by collectors (mildly put), a bit of space in the book shall nevertheless be given also to a few ladies' pocket watches.

Above: four ladies' open face pocket watches in comparison to a men's watch on the top of normal size.

Like the ladies' wristwatches, the vintage ladies' pocket watches also receive little or no attention amongst watch collectors. Malicious gossip has it, that watchmakers use them to throw after customers who forgot to close the door.

Women, in their majority, are less into collecting used watches, at least not to an extend of becoming a hoarding freak. For the men, they are, in their major part, simply too small and technically not very interesting.

In view of a broader coverage of timepieces in the collection, it doesn't hurt to add also a few of those little sisters of 'real' pocket watches; after all, they usually come along relatively cheap, and if this is still too much for you, just leave the door open, next time you leave the shop of your watchmaker …

Left and below (all images): ladies' open face pocket watch, silver, approx. 1860, alpine dial, cylinder escapement, key wind and -set (in the back), 10 jewels *(I see the marking well, but lack Faith's constant trust')*, Ø 37mm. Hallmarks in the case and on the pendant show a crab, a French guarantee of fineness for small objects (silver content 0.800).

Left (both images): ladies' open face pocket watch, approx. 1920 to 1930, silver red gold plated, enameled dial, cylinder escapement, stem (crown) wind and –set (pin set variant), Ø 31mm.

Hallmarks: Imperial Crown and crescent moon, the German silver mark = 0.800 silver, also a grouse, the Swiss silver mark = 0.800 silver, gilded silver bezel 'galonne', initials AH and PG.

Engravings inner cover: 'Remontoir Cylindre 10 Rubis'. Now, this is another flapdoodle-designation. Leaving aside the alleged 10 jewels: in the true sense of a remontoir technique, the mainspring does not directly deliver the power, but frequently reloads an interim power source, which gives a more constant force to the escapement. Here, this designation has been degenerated to describe a simple stem winding of a normal mainspring. Well, if you take the human winder as the prime power source and the mainspring as the interim, that is even correct.

Above (both images): ladies' open face pocket watch, approx. 1925, Swiss, enameled dial, cylinder escapement, stem (crown) wind and -set (pin-set version), Ø 38mm. Gun metal case (a copper-zinc-tin alloy with small parts of lead and nickel): Even the ladies' watches often had cases made from cheaper materials, especially during economically difficult times.

Quartz watches have already made their appearance on the market and a lot of movements, intended originally for mechanical wristwatches, found a new use, not only in small ladies' pocket watches, but also in larger men's pocket watches, with a wide spacer inside, holding it in place, and a prolonged winding stem. This one here went into a ladies' pocket watch:

Above (both images): ladies' open face pocket watch, STOWA, Germany, last quarter of the 20th century, lever escapement, stem (crown) wind and –set. Case gold 0.585. The movement was made by FHF – Fabrique d'Horologerie de Fontainemelon, Switzerland, FHF cal. 69 (produced as from 1976, mainly for wristwatches), Incabloc shock protection, f = 21,600 A/h, Ø 35mm.

Above (both images): open face ladies pocket watch for a necklace, **VALGINE, Swiss 1980s**, movement Peseux cal. 7040 (normally used in wristwatches), lever escapement, 17 jewels, f = 21,600 A/h, stem (crown) wind and –set, Ø34mm.

Stopwatches: watches cannot only tell the time, but also measure shorter time intervals; nothing new since the invention of the water clock or the hourglass, just a bit refined in later days.

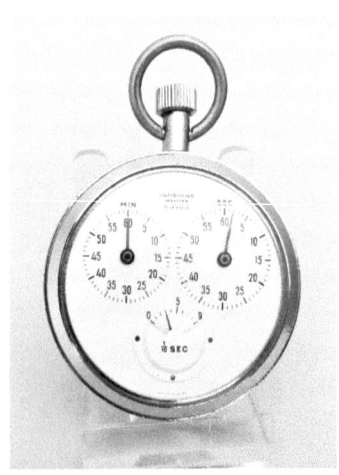

Left: **JUNGHANS, Germany, stop watch, early 1960s**, from the 'Meister' (master) series, movement Junghans cal. 628/1, with indications for 1/10th of a second.

Junghans, which once became the largest watch producing company in the world in the year 1903, was also developing some ingenious stopwatches, technically ahead of their time.

This reliable movement caliber was already developed in the year 1930.

In the middle of the 1950s, they came out with the 'Dreikreis' (three dials) Meister stopwatch, caliber 28 and 628. For the first time, it was possible to take a reading of tenth of a second, with a full seconds indication and a period up to 60 minutes.

The movement caliber 28/11, which followed, was the answer of Junghans to the 'Mikrograph' made by Heuer, which both could measure hundreds of a second. With a total measurement period of 12 minutes, Junghans had set a new record at the time.

My name is ROLEX, Victor Rolex... At the end, an example of a **'frankenwatch'**. 'Fake' (total forgery), 're-dial' (re-done dial, often looking like an effort gone wrong with a children's stamping set) or 'franken' (a watch cobbled together from various parts not originally belonging together), there is an ocean of this trash floating around, mostly on Internet selling platforms. The collector has to be extremely cautious not to end up with one of those sickening products.

Re-dials are certainly acceptable to some extent, if done professionally, especially, if a seller openly states that a dial has been re-done. Fakes are totally out, even when things are clear, unless you want to run around as a pitiful boaster, matching the watch to your fake Prada shoes.

But also Franken-watches, if not intentionally assembled to screw people, can have a serious background, but this is only very, very rarely the case. The following example was an attempt to bring a movement back into operation, whose case went into the melting pot along with the gold-rush.

Above (both images): open face franken- pocket watch, high-grade Swiss movement, approx. 1925, compensating balance/screw balance, Breguet spiral, stem (crown) wind and –set, screwed chatons, very special fine-regulation, decentral seconds indication, case nickel, Ø 50mm. Hands do not match, the enameled dial might have originally been with the movement, or not. The case is a little too large. As there was not enough room for a spacer, one of the prime tools of horology, wooden tooth-picks (yes, you are reading correctly!) had to do the job. They can be used to give the balance wheel a little push or to stir around in the movement, without scratching too much. They are also (perhaps secretly brought along) ideal for pre-inspections at auctions. Here, a few toothpicks were pressed between the movement and case, and the excess was cut off.

WATCH MOVEMENTS – THE GOLD RUSH

The constant rise of the gold prices meant the end for many watches whose cases were made of that precious metal.

When watches housed in golden case are to be sold, offers usually do not exceed much the pure material value of the gold content. Collectors want to collect watches, not gold, and the price for a watch with a case from this costly material, is often much too high anyway and the interest in a particular piece is mostly lost, especially if the seller also wants to have a substantial surcharge for the watch itself.

Selling watches is a much more complicated and time-consuming thing than fast cash against gold. The gold purchasers are interested only in the gold, a quick deal and not in the collector's value of a watch. Prices on the precious metal markets fluctuate and watches are not their business and time spent here can be better allocated to their core activities.

It is, of course, a different story with the absolute high-end watches, but even such precious timepieces, for instance from Lange und Soehne, have disappeared, when the gold cases went into the East Block to be converted into dental gold.

Very often, clueless sellers were even surprised by the allegedly high offers. Most of them, however, are much disappointed that they cannot get much more than the material gold value. After some time spent looking for a buyer, they finally go to the gold purchasers, where everything goes fast and uncomplicated. A collector, possibly paying a higher price, has to be found at first, cash might not be coming forward so quickly and then, there are these endless discussions about the state of the watch, a necessary service or repair and whatever, with a price finally talked down below the gold value of the case. For the gold purchaser, the condition of the watch and its movement is of little or no interest.

The gold purchaser most does not have the know-how to professionally remove the movement from the case. It also does not make much sense in view of the expenditure of time. And then, the selling of the bare movement is not so easygoing. It would have to be described in detail, and finally, the packaging and shipping is a delicate and also time-consuming matter. So, the movements are mostly knocked out with a hammer or excavated with a pair of pliers.

Nevertheless, some movements (with or without dials and hands) have survived – in whatever condition. The crown and the winding stem are often gone, like the pin-mechanism, usually integrated in the outer part of the case. Winding (and setting) is no longer possible.

But occasionally, some people have enough experience (or luck) with the removal of movements, or the sellers have done this themselves, halfway professional, before the case went to into the melting pot.

Such movements can usually be bought at reasonable prices. They are ideal objects of study or practice. The function of the mechanics at work can be well observed, at home or on the desk in the office, possibly in a nice display case.

Unless it is something very rare and antique, they should be complete with dial, hands, crown and stem (if not key-wind and set). The pin-set mechanism is part of the case, but you can work with a blunt toothpick if necessary.

The following movements are shown without any specific description. They all have been in gold cases and are of high quality for their time, revealing some real technical tidbits.

Above (both images): movement from a ladies' wristwatch, ETA caliber 2412. The watch from which this movement was taken had a sales price of around US $20,000.00. It is the smallest movement ETA has ever made, smaller than 1 US- or Euro Cent. Case and wristband, both made of gold, were sold as well as the diamonds set on the dial. The seller had sent this movement by mail, wrapped in a paper tissue and in a normal envelope. It has survived these *'tortures'* and runs extremely well.

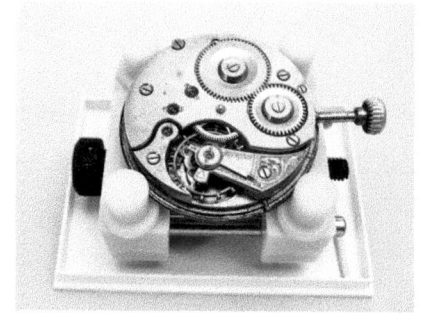

Above (both images): With a plastic mineral collector's box around, the movement is protected, and it is also an ideal way to put it on display and see it doing its work, at home or on the desk in the office.

Below: left face, right movement side:

Below: left face, right movement side:

147

Also available, the book dealing with Radium, Tritium and other radioactive substances contained in the luminous paint on dial and hands of vintage watches and the dangers arising therefrom:

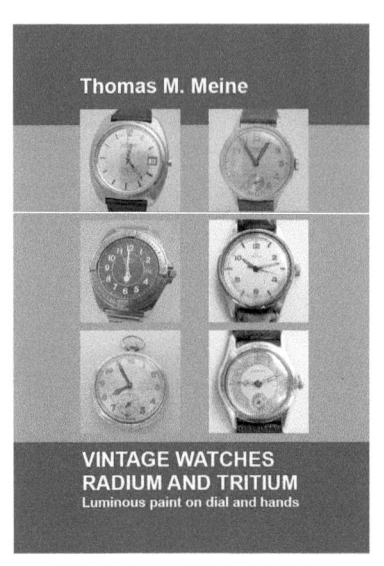

ISBN: 9 783752 821406